353

DEALS, DEALS,
and More DEALS

I hope you enjoy
my story.

Jnownichols

OKLAHOMA *TRACKMAKER* SERIES

DEALS, DEALS, *and More* DEALS

The Life of John W. Nichols

by
BOB BURKE

foreword by
DAVID L. BOREN

series editor
Gini Moore Campbell

associate editors
Eric Dabney and Stephanie Ayala

OKLAHOMA
HERITAGE
ASSOCIATION
Oklahoma City

Printed in the United States of America.
ISBN 1-885596-26-X
Library of Congress Catalog Number 2004112147
Book cover and contents designed by Sandi Welch/www.2WDesignGroup.com
Unless otherwise noted, photographs are courtesy of the John W. and Mary Nichols Family.

CONTENTS

ACKNOWLEDGMENTS

John W. *Nichols is a humble man.* When discussing his Herculean achievements in life, John often says he "accidentally" discovered an industry-changing method of funding oil exploration, he "accidentally" met lovely Mary, his wife and companion of 67 years, or that he "accidentally" met people who became invaluable connections in his innovative and highly lucrative business deals.

However, my research reached one conclusion—John W. Nichols did nothing by accident. It was his hard work, brilliance in business, dedication, and dependence on God for guidance that simply put him at the right place—at the right time—for his entire life.

I am thankful to many people whose stories added to this book. John and Mary and their three wonderful children and their families opened their hearts and photograph albums. Grandson Randy Street provided his incredible genealogical research. Dr. Odie Faulk's early interviews and Dr. Kenny Franks' work on the manuscript made it much easier to complete the project. Interviews were conducted with Terry Barrett, Susan Ketch, Bill Avery, Bob Heston, Helen Hilseweck, Tommy Leflett, Gary Fuller, Bill Majors, Dee Loos, Dorothy McDonald, Michael Robertson, Michael Taylor, Tom Ferguson, Norman Benzaquen, John W. Fisher, Peter Grunebaum, John van Merkensteijn, III,

Betty and David Street, Larry and Polly Nichols, H.R. Sanders, Jr., and Kent and Diane Nichols.

Thanks to Darla Neuendorf, Ginger Armstrong, Cindy Banks, Susan Ketch, Shea Snyder, and Karen Ponder for editorial assistance; to Anna Hubbard for help with photographs; and to Linda Lynn, Mary Phillips, Melissa Hayer, Robin Davison, and Billie Harry at the archives of *The Daily Oklahoman*.

I appreciate the efforts of series editor Gini Moore Campbell and the Oklahoma Heritage Association for its consistent commitment to preserve Oklahoma's bold and exciting story.

—Bob Burke

FOREWORD

by David L. Boren

It has been said that as we come to know other people, their lives "rub off" on us. All of those who have come to know John Nichols have had their lives enriched as a result. I am one of those fortunate ones who have been privileged to share a friendship with John Nichols and with Mary Nichols, his wife and partner of more than 67 years. On the following pages Bob Burke captures the spirit and life experiences of this remarkable man.

Much can be learned about how to live a meaningful life by reading about the life of John Nichols. He was born in 1914 in Ardmore, Oklahoma. He had the benefit of a good public education and took full advantage of it to prepare himself for college. At the University of Oklahoma he worked his way through college waiting tables at a fraternity house. He pledged Delta Tau Delta and became the natural leader of his local chapter and was later national president. He made countless numbers of friends because he was a genuine friend to others. He cared about others and extended himself for them. He took full advantage of his university years and sought out excellent courses from outstanding professors who influenced his life.

A man of deep personal religious faith, he was known from his earliest years as a person of integrity whose word was his bond and who was at peace with himself.

Throughout his life he has given back generously to the institutions which helped shape his life and opportunities including his church and his alma mater, the University of Oklahoma. He has been especially generous in giving scholarships because he never forgot his own personal effort to obtain an education.

After graduating from the university, Nichols worked briefly on the floor of the New York Stock Exchange during the depression years seeing first hand how financial tides can change. He went to work as a public accountant in Oklahoma City in 1936. In his practice which included work for several local oil companies, he learned a great deal about that business. He used what he learned, including his knowledge of tax laws, to create the world's first oil and gas drilling fund registered with the Securities and Exchange Commission. His leadership profoundly changed the way that drilling programs were funded in this country until Congress restructured tax laws in 1986.

With F. G. Blackwood, John Nichols built a large regional oil and gas company in the 1950s and 1960s. In 1970, he founded Devon Energy Corporation which grew to become the largest United States producer of oil and natural gas. It is no wonder that a prominent national publication listed him as one of the "One Hundred Most Influential Leaders in the Petroleum Industry in the Twentieth Century."

Through all of his activities, which included business travel around the world long after he passed the age of 80, John Nichols always found time for his family, especially his grandchildren. He took each of them individually on special trips with him to Europe and other places. He passed on to them his deep religious faith and his love of history. He also passed on his love of great books, a love that he shares with his wife Mary and which motivated them to establish a collection of rare books at the Bizzell Memorial Library at the University of Oklahoma. He also passed on his love of the arts. John and Mary Nichols have made many gifts to O.U.'s School of Dance and helped organize three international conferences on Business and the Arts for the university.

The marriage of John and Mary Nichols is extraordinary by any measure. Sweethearts in their college years, they have supported each other, loved each other, inspired each other, shared many intellectual interests, and worked as partners in philanthropic endeavors of historic proportions.

In short, the story of John Nichols is in many ways uniquely American. It describes the qualities that have made this a great and special country. History illustrates the importance of strong public education from the earliest years of childhood through the university years so that all young people like the young man from Ardmore, Oklahoma, will have an equal opportunity to equip themselves for life. It describes the work ethic, the courage to take risks, and the creative entrepreneurial spirit which have given vitality to our society. John's life illustrates the importance of bedrock spiritual values and the meaning that is given to life by giving back to others. Those are the values that led the Frenchman Alexis de Tocqueville to write almost 200 years ago that "America is great because America is good." His life also teaches us that the way to preserve our most important values is to nurture the institutions which pass them on to the next generation, especially the family, the church, the school, and the university.

America will remain a great nation as long as we continue to have men and women like John and Mary Nichols and as long as we give them the opportunities to develop their talents and live by their values. The life of John Nichols challenges each of us to follow his example of honoring the past by passing on enhanced opportunities to the generations which will follow us.

David L. Boren is President of the University of Oklahoma. He previously served Oklahoma as Governor and United States Senator.

PROLOGUE

·····························

"**I** *know he's a crook*, but I can't figure out how he's crooked," quipped meat packing magnate Phillip Armour as he introduced his new friend, John W. Nichols, a 35-year-old Oklahoma City, Oklahoma, accountant. Armour also called Nichols a "highbinder" in his introduction. It was a half century later that Nichols discovered highbinders were Chinese immigrants to California who enforced their blackmail and criminal activities with the use of knives, swords, clubs, and hatchets.

The swarthy introduction did not intimidate Nichols who had been invited to explain his new oil and gas investment tax shelter plan to some of Armour's friends. A week before, Armour was so impressed with Nichols' plan, the first ever of its kind approved by the Securities and Exchange Commission, he wrote a $100,000 check on the spot.

Armour's friends, who had gathered at the exclusive University Club in Chicago, Illinois, were captains of American industry and were plagued by oppressive federal tax laws that took as much as 90 percent of their income. Nichols had insisted that no one attend the meeting unless they were in the 90 percent tax bracket and that they bring their financial planners and tax lawyers with them.

It was a prestigious group sitting around linen-draped tables in the private dining room in the meeting place for the rich and famous in the Loop area of the Windy City. The meeting was chaired by Nichols' associate, Clinton Davidson.

From Milwaukee, Wisconsin, came Alfred Uihleins, president of Schlitz Brewing Company. Others present were K.T. Keller, president of Chrysler Motors; Benjamin Fairless, chairman of Bethlehem Steel; Alex Nason, founder of Luberzhal Corporation, a major supplier of lubricants for the oil industry; Herbert Johnson of S.C. Johnson & Son, Inc., makers of Johnson Wax and hundreds of other products; and John Pillsbury, president of the Pillsbury food product empire.

The executives, dressed in fine tailored suits and chewing on expensive Cuban cigars, were desperate in their search for ways to keep more of their income. "I'm looking for some way to keep more than 10 percent," one CEO said. They had come to the right place on a chilly Monday in January, 1951.

Nichols carefully outlined his completely legal and above board plan. He explained how his joint venture could provide large amounts of tax free income. The depletion allowance of 27.5 percent, the tax code's allowance of production expenses in the year which they occurred, and the fact that there was no alternative minimum income tax were the core elements of Nichols' proposal. He told the executives that intangible expenses often made up 70 percent of the cost of a successful well and John showed them a diagram that proved his plan resulted in little taxable income for the investors.

Nichols assured his audience that he always played by the rules—but oil and gas exploration provided almost unlimited potential to use the burdensome tax laws to the advantage of investors. With hardly any questions from those assembled, Nichols explained how his plan could almost miraculously save high-income investors up to half their annual income tax bill.

The industrial giants listened in awe with occasional glances at their financial wizards who took copious notes and nodded in agreement with Nichols' assessment of the anti-business climate that existed, courtesy of federal tax laws. For more than an hour Nichols laid out the legality, originality, and potential of his deal that some called "a promoter's dream."

The ball was clearly in the court of the business leaders gathered in the Windy City. Following his presentation, Nichols said, "There is no pressure here. I won't call you—but if you're interested, call me."

After the corporate leaders huddled with their experts, they invited Nichols to visit their offices in distant cities to talk further about reducing the sting of their tax bills. Within weeks, each of the high-income industrialists committed hard cash to Nichols' plan that he called Fund 1. Within a short time, Nichols raised $1,430,000 from investors, including movie stars Dick Powell, Ginger Rogers, Barbara Stanwyck, and Robert Taylor, and a Chinese investor who handed over $300,000 cash in a suitcase.

The results of the joint venture tax-sheltered investment were unbelievable. For example, a half-century later, heirs of the Pillsbury fortune receive nearly $17,000 per month on their grandfather's original $50,000 investment.

The revolutionary plan developed by the innovative young Oklahoma City accountant changed the way that America's oil and gas fields would be developed in the second half of the 20th century. It earned John W. Nichols a special place in the hall of fame of American ingenuity.

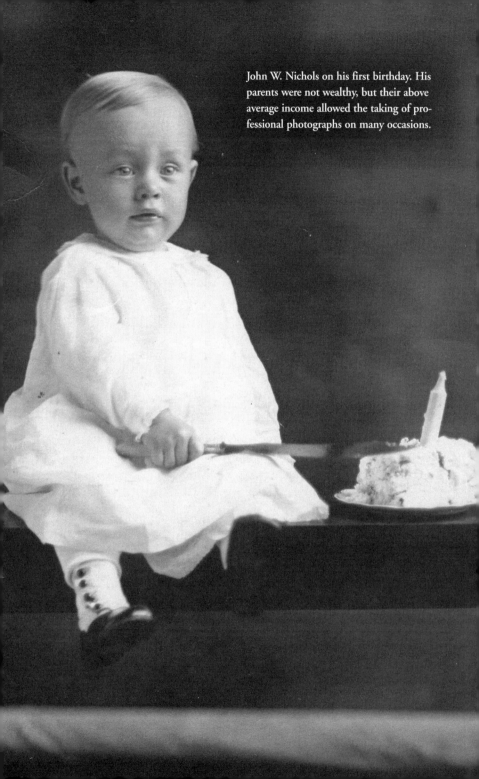

John W. Nichols on his first birthday. His parents were not wealthy, but their above average income allowed the taking of professional photographs on many occasions.

Ardmore Beginnings

I was the only kid on the block with a bicycle.
JOHN W. NICHOLS

T**he work ethic and legendary business acumen** of John W. Nichols was in his blood. His grandfather, Andrew Hunter Nichols, born in Kentucky in 1844, was a successful insurance broker and owned a dry goods store in Whitesboro, Texas, in the 1870s. Whitesboro was a booming north Texas frontier town where shootings were common. But by 1880, the town had a newspaper, a bank, and regular train service from the Missouri, Kansas, and Texas Railroad, commonly called the Katy.

In 1880, John Tutt "John T." Nichols was born in Whitesboro. At the age of 12, his father died and it became necessary for John T. to find employment. Whitesboro had a population of only 1,000 and job opportunities were nonexistent. As a result, John T. moved 15 miles to the west and found employment at the Tyler Simpson Wholesale Grocery Company in Gainesville, Texas. His mother stayed in Whitesboro to care for her three younger children.

ABOVE: The Carter County Courthouse opened in 1910—just in time for the oil rush. Courtesy Oklahoma Publishing Company.

Gainesville, established in 1850, grew slowly because of frequent Indian attacks. But after the Civil War, the town prospered, primarily because of local merchants selling goods to cattle drovers on the Chisholm Trail. A second boom of population and business activity came to Gainesville in 1886 when the Atchison, Topeka, and Santa Fe Railroad arrived. High cotton prices and plenty of rain fueled the local economy. By 1892, nearly 5,000 people called Gainesville their home.

Thanks to its railroad connections, Gainesville was a wholesale and retail center for several counties in north Texas and southern Indian Territory. The Tyler Simpson Wholesale Grocery Company bought fresh food from local producers and canned goods from far off suppliers for distribution to small grocery

Carter County farmers waiting to deliver their wagonloads of cotton at a cotton gin in Ardmore in 1910. Cotton was king in southern Oklahoma at the beginning of the 20th century. Courtesy Ardmore Public Library.

stores within a reasonable radius of Gainesville. Simpson's sales-men traveled their routes across the region by train, buggy, and horseback. Most of the small stores in tiny communities and hamlets ordered less than $25 worth of groceries per week, but there were so many stores, the Simpsons prospered.

John T. had the lowest job in the Tyler Simpson warehouse. When a salesman brought orders in, John T. and other work-ers filled them and loaded the goods onto a wagon or railroad freight car. He worked twelve-hour days, six days a week. The economic panic that gripped the country in 1893 made his job that much more precious. With many out of work, John T. worked at a fast pace to assure his continued employment. With his long work hours, 13-year-old John T. had no time for formal schoolwork in the Gainesville schools. However, he received an excellent practical education in the fundamentals of human nature and business.[1]

In 1900, Tyler Simpson Wholesale Grocery expanded east by opening a warehouse in Tyler, Texas, and north, into Indian Territory, by building a distribution warehouse in Ardmore. The southern part of Indian Territory was bustling with activity in anticipation of the end of Indian tribal sovereignty and the influx of white settlers.

Ardmore was founded in 1887 in the Chickasaw Nation when the Santa Fe Railroad laid tracks north from Gainesville and opened a station on what had been a prairie. A small town grew as a supply and marketing point, first for local cattlemen and then for cotton farmers who swarmed into the region.

In 1898, Ardmore was incorporated, bringing new businesses such as Tyler Simpson Grocery to the area. When the St. Louis and San Francisco Railroad, the Frisco, came through Ardmore in 1902, a boom was on. By 1904, Ardmore, with a population of more than 10,000, was the largest city in Indian Territory.

The Whiteman family around 1900. Sitting, left to right, Lillian Whiteman, who became John W.'s favorite aunt, Henry Whiteman, Ted Whiteman, and the matriarch of the family, Bertha Taylor Whiteman. Standing, left to right, Charles Whiteman, William Whiteman, John W.'s mother, Mary Whiteman, John Whiteman, and Taylor Whiteman. Bertha Taylor Whiteman, John W.'s grandmother, buried her silver in the back yard to hide it from the Yankees during the Civil War. She was killed in an auto accident in 1932.

John Tutt Nichols on his 87th birthday. He died at age 90 in 1970 in Oklahoma City.

To open its warehouse in Ardmore, Tyler Simpson Grocery sent an experienced manager and, as his assistant, John T. Nichols, a seasoned 20-year-old veteran of the wholesale grocery business. Even before John T. arrived in Indian Territory, he was assured of a place to stay. Arthur Simpson, one of the owners of Tyler Simpson Grocery, had a brother, Burton "Burt" Simpson, an Ardmore businessman. Before John T. left Gainesville, Art Simpson wrote his brother to ask if he could find a place for his young worker to live.[2]

Burt Simpson was involved in the fledging oil business in Ardmore. He was married to Lillian Whiteman, whose brother, John Whiteman, had been his partner for a year in the Whiteman-Simpson Department Store in Ardmore.

Soon, several members of the Whiteman family lived in Ardmore, including John Whiteman; his brothers, Will and Charles; his sister, Lillian Simpson; and Lillian's mother, Bertha Taylor Whiteman, whose husband had recently died in Dallas, Texas.

The Whiteman family had arrived in the New World from Europe in the early 1700s and had lived for generations in St. Francisville and Jackson, Louisiana. A flourishing family business was decimated by conflict over loyalties in the Civil War—four Whiteman brothers joined the Confederate Army.

It was in Bertha Whiteman's home where John T. Nichols was allowed to rent a room. Living in the same house was Bertha's daughter, Mary. The daily contact, and the discovery that they had so much in common, brought Mary and John T. together romantically. They fell in love and were married in 1905.

Continuing his employment at Tyler Simpson Wholesale Grocery, John T. was able to buy a vacant lot

RIGHT: John Tutt Nichols moved to Ardmore with the Simpson Wholesale Grocery Company.

LEFT: Bertha Taylor Whiteman, John W. Nichols' grandmother, was a frequent babysitter for John W. After her husband, Charles Patterson Whiteman, died in Texas she moved to Ardmore to be close to her family. Bertha read stories to John W. when he was ill. Charles Whiteman fought for the Confederacy in the Civil War and was held for two years by Union soldiers as a prisoner of war.[6]

James Warren Taylor, John W. Nichols' great grandfather, was born in Virginia in 1816. He later moved to Louisiana and married Mary Hill Pipes. Both had large inheritances from their fathers. They purchased a large cotton plantation called Woodlawn. At one time, Taylor was the largest slave owner in Louisiana, with more than 900 indentured servants. This photograph was taken in 1889 when Taylor was 73 years old. He died in 1903 at the age of 87.

Woodlawn was the name of the Louisiana plantation home of James Warren Taylor. It was built before the Civil War, circa 1850. The home had three floors and high ceilings. In the hallway on the first floor sat an elaborate silver water pitcher and cups, an heirloom that has been passed down to John W. Nichols. When Woodlawn was sold to the State of Louisiana for preservation as a historic site, the adjacent family cemetery was reserved for use by the Taylor family. The home, in East Feliciana Parish, is still open for public tours.

and build a house at 329 G Street Southwest in Ardmore. A few months after he and his bride moved into the new home, the house next door caught fire, the fire spread, and the Nichols home was burned to the ground. John T. had the house rebuilt but it was destroyed by fire a second time two years later when oily rags in a closet caught fire. Fortunately, no one was injured in either fire and the Nichols rebuilt a third time.

John T.'s future at Tyler Simpson Grocery was limited. He realized that if he wanted a better job with better pay, he had to look elsewhere. He found his brighter future in the cotton brokerage business and went to work for Neely Dodson.[4]

In the early years of the 20th century, Ardmore was the largest inland cotton center in America. Several cotton gins processed the thousands of bales grown by farmers within wagon distance of Ardmore. Thirteen foreign brokers and many local brokers bargained for the right to buy the outstanding quality cotton grown in the fertile soil along the Red River.[5]

When harvest season arrived, cotton bales were stacked along the length of Main Street on both sides. Farmers,

May Tutt, the grandmother of John W. Nichols. May was devoted to music and taught piano in school for many years. The Tutts came from Missouri where Colonel Andrew M. Tutt was a respected attorney in Clinton, Missouri, in the middle of the 19th century. Colonel Tutt, fighting for the Confederacy, was killed in the Battle of Pea Ridge in Arkansas during the Civil War. John W. Nichols traces his lineage through the Tutts back to the Middle Ages, to the era's most famous ruler, Charlemagne, and down through William the Conqueror and Henry II of England.[7]

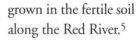

with their loaded wagons of fluffy white cotton, waited in lines that sometimes stretched three miles for their turn at one of the local gins.

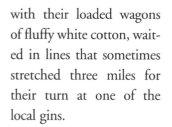

RIGHT: Mary Whitman Nichols, John W.'s mother.

BELOW: John Tutt and Mary Whiteman Nichols on their 50th wedding anniversary in 1955.

Cotton was king of the Ardmore area economy. Each spring, merchants extended credit to cotton farmers with the expectation that they would be repaid when the harvest came, the cotton was ginned, and the bales sold to local or foreign brokers. When the weather and prices were good, everyone prospered. But, when drought hit and cotton withered in the field, farmers had little or no cotton to gin and merchants were left with unpaid bills.

Cotton prices had generally been high in the decade preceding Oklahoma statehood in 1907. As prices fell, Ardmore leaders looked to diversify their economy. Their answer was the discovery of oil that soon would take the region by storm and make millionaires out of oil field workers and property owners alike.[8]

For more than 25 years, there had been talk of oil in western Carter County. In fact, a man named Palmer drilled a 420-feet well in 1888. Newspaper accounts said oil began "oozing and slopping" over the top of the hole. However, the Wirt Franklin No. 1, the area's first commercial well, was completed on August 4, 1913.[9]

News of the discovery of a paying oil well spread quickly. Within three months 14 oil companies held leases in what became known as the Healdton Field. Ardmore, as the largest city near the discovery, quickly became home to oil companies and independent producers, and for drillers and roughnecks. The city boomed as supply firms built offices and storage yards and entrepreneurs erected plush hotels and new stores.[10]

Because the cotton brokerage business was seasonal, John T. Nichols had much of the year to work with Burt Simpson, who was taking full advantage of opportunities offered in the oil business. John T. worked long hours and drove many miles, chasing leases and reporting on oil drilling activity.

Left to right, Bertha Taylor Whiteman, John W.'s grandmother; Mary Whiteman Nichols, his mother; and Aunt Lillian Whiteman Simpson.

One night, John T. was driving his Model T Ford near Healdton in a rainstorm along a stretch of road that was frequented by highwaymen who often robbed, and even killed, unwary travelers. Because of the threat, John T. carried a pistol in a pocket he had made in the door of the Model T.[11]

Buckets of rain made the unpaved road a quagmire. As John T. struggled to keep the car on the road, he came upon a hitchhiker huddled along the muddy road. Spurning his thoughts of safety, John T. stopped his car and offered the hitchhiker a ride. A few minutes into the ride, John T. asked if the hitchhiker knew the time. When the man pulled a watch from his pocket, John T. thought he had been the victim of a pickpocket and yelled, "That's my watch!" He pulled his pistol from its hiding place and demanded of the hitchhiker, "Give me the watch and get out of the car." The hitchhiker, despite the pouring rain outside, handed over the watch and stepped into the rainy night.

John T. drove on home and finally got to bed. The next morning, he told his wife about the hitchhiker and bragged that he had gotten his watch back. His startled wife said, "You left your watch on the dresser yesterday!" The hitchhiker story was not mentioned again for many years.

John T. was not among Ardmore's new oil millionaires like Burt Simpson because he had not followed Simpson's lead in buying land under which petroleum was found. However, John T. was a prosperous, middle class businessmen who was well thought of in the community. He and his wife, Mary, were regulars at Ardmore's First Presbyterian Church, and he was an active member of several civic and fraternal organizations. He was especially active in the local Masonic Lodge and eventually became a 32nd degree Mason.[12]

John T. was also a member of the Ardmore Elks Lodge. The Elks, the common name of the Benevolent and Protective Order of Elks, was a fraternal and charitable organization formed in 1868 in New York City. Membership was limited to United States citizens at least 21 years old who believed in God. The purpose of the group was to give scholarships, medical aid, and assistance to the American Red Cross, needy veterans, crippled children, and

John W. Nichols
at age two.

both Boy Scouts and Girl Scouts. Several times, the Ardmore Elks
sent John T. as a delegate to the national convention. In 1915, he
served as Exalted Ruler of the Ardmore Elks Lodge.

John T. and Mary had been married nine years when they
became the parents of a boy on November 6, 1914. They named

John W. Nichols, center, is flanked by his next door neighbor twins, Fred and Fain Crockett. The Crockett family lived on one side of the Nichols in Ardmore—on the other side lived the family of Robert A. Hefner, later a Justice of the Oklahoma Supreme Court.

him John Whiteman Nichols—John, after his father—and Whiteman, his mother's maiden name.

At the age of eight months, John W.'s photograph appeared in a Los Angeles, California, newspaper account of the national Elks convention. The caption under John W.'s photograph read, "Youngest Member of Elkdom." The story said John W. had accompanied his parents all the way from Oklahoma and surely held all records for youthful attendance at such an affair. The reporter called him "Johnnie Nichols" and predicted that 40 years hence the lad would surely be running for Exalted Ruler. The adult Elks at the convention were so taken by the baby boy that they have made him a life member and presented their gift on a silver plate.[13]

John W.'s early education came at home where his mundane questions were given serious answers. He also learned from Sunday

The Nichols on vacation at Seven Falls near Colorado Springs, Colorado, in 1918. Left to right, friend Harry Crockett, John W. Nichols, John T. Nichols, Mrs. Crockett, and Mary Nichols.

school and on family outings to see the silent movies of the day. He was too young to understand his parents' discussions each night at dinner about the ravages of World War I and, closer to home, the great influenza epidemic that killed many people throughout the world, including several dozen people in Carter County.

When John W. was five, he accompanied his father and mother on a business trip to Europe.

John W. and his mother on their trip to Europe in 1920.

John T. wanted to see the major battlefields of the Great War that had just ended. He put a helmet on his son and took a photograph of him standing on a bombed-out tank.

John W.'s most vivid memory of the trip to Europe is on board the ship sailing the Atlantic Ocean. He was playing with a little girl about his same age when his hat blew off and disappeared in the choppy waters. More than eighty years after the event, John said, "I can still see that cap blowing off—forever gone—into the ocean."[14]

When the Nichols family arrived back in Ardmore, John W.'s uncle, Burt Simpson, surprised him with a new 20-inch bicycle. John W. was very grateful—he was the only child on the block with a bicycle.

Formal education for John W. began at Ardmore's Third Ward School, a red brick structure about three blocks from the Nichols

John W. Nichols was introduced to the game of golf at an early age. In this photograph, he tries out his "drive" on the Dornick Hills Country Club course that was under construction at the time north of Ardmore. On top of the cliff in the background was the green for hole # 7. John W.'s father had him wade a creek to recover balls that went astray.

home. John W. and neighborhood friends walked to school each day. Soon, his favorite pastime was marbles. The boys drew a large circle and each placed the same number of marbles in the circle. The game was called "keeps" because each boy took turns shooting and kept the marbles he knocked outside the circle.

The Nichols' next door neighbor was Robert A. Hefner who had been elected mayor of Ardmore in 1920. The Hefner's youngest child was William Johnson "Bill" Hefner, a few months younger than John W. Bill was larger in stature than John W. and often beat him up. When John W. would show up for supper with a bloody nose, his mother or grandmother would say, "You've got to stand up and defend yourself." John W. took the advice to heart one day when he picked up a hoe and hit Bill in the head, requiring stitches at the local hospital. After that fight, Bill and John W. became close friends until the Hefners moved to Oklahoma City in 1926.

Mary Nichols enjoyed being a mother to John W. When he arrived home from school each day, she greeted him with cookies and milk and questions about his day. In the summers, his parents took him to the circus. Ardmore was relatively safe for children to walk by themselves to downtown movie theaters where John W. could see cowboys chasing rustlers, pilots in aerial combat, and sheiks racing across the desert—all for a nickel.

It was with Bill Hefner that John W. got into the only serious trouble that plagued his pre-teen years. One day his mother was having a party and had baked an angel food cake. Bill and John W. ate the entire cake before Mrs. Nichols' guests arrived.

John W. spent a great deal of time with members of his mother's family. At Christmas, his Aunt Lillian served as hostess for lavish holiday celebrations. With oil money, Lillian and Burt Simpson had built a huge home just two blocks from the Nichols home. The house had a four-car garage and a five-foot

John W. Nichols on vacation with his parents in Colorado in 1928.

John W. Nichols' graduation picture at Ardmore High School.

brick fence around the large yard. The dining room seated 30 people and the Simpsons had several house servants and a cook. In the summer months, Aunt Lillian often escaped the sultry southern Oklahoma weather and vacationed in California.

Once when John W. was playing tag at Aunt Lillian's home, he climbed upon the gate of a five-foot-high brick fence and fell, breaking his arm. He was taken to Hardy Sanitarium, where Dr. Walter Hardy set the break. However, it did not heal properly and for the remainder of his life his arm was slightly crooked.

In 1924, John T. Nichols was transferred to Atlanta, Georgia, headquarters of Westpoint Mills, for whom he had been buying cotton. For almost two years, during his fifth and part of his sixth grades, John W. rode his bicycle to Spring Street School near downtown Atlanta before his family returned to Ardmore.

When John W. was older, he joined his father on the golf course of the Ardmore Country Club, Dornick Hills, and in high school played on the school's golf team. He finished second in the 1929 Class E State Amateur Tournament. In 1932, John W. lost in the final round of the State Tournament to Walter Emery of Duncan, Oklahoma, who eventually became one of the state's most noted amateur golfers.

John W. also joined Boy Scout Troop Four in Ardmore, sponsored by the Presbyterian Church. During the summers, he attended summer camp and stayed in the Hefner Lodge at Camp Chapman in the Arbuckle Mountains. It was at Boy Scout camp that John W. met lifelong friend B.C. Clark, Jr., whose father was a prominent jeweler in Purcell. The boys enjoyed camp, especially the 14-mile round-trip hike to nearby Turner Falls. When John W. was 14, he completed the requirements for Eagle Scout.

Much of the social life in high school of John W. and his best friend, Joe Somerville, revolved around the First Presbyterian Church's Christian Endeavor group, which met on Sunday evenings.[15]

The highlights of John W.'s high school years were summer vacations either to Colorado or to Long Beach, California, where Aunt Lillian leased an apartment. John W. served as an escort for his aunt and grandmother as they rode the Atchison, Topeka, and Santa Fe Railroad Santa Fe Chief across the American Southwest. Although Aunt Lillian kept a Buick automobile in California, she did not like to drive, and John W. served as the family driver.

In May, 1932, John W. graduated from Ardmore High School and was faced with the decision of where to attend college and what he would study. He settled on the University of Oklahoma and accounting.

But before John W. began his college career, his father landed him a job as a messenger boy for Fenner and Beane on Wall Street in New York City. Fenner and Beane was a predecessor to Merrill Lynch. John T. Nichols knew the principals of the firm from his cotton brokerage dealings with the Fenner and Beane office in New Orleans.

John W. went by train and stopped in Chicago for a day on his way to New York City. His father rented him an apartment in Rye, New York, the last train stop before entering Connecticut. Each weekday morning, John W. took the train to Grand Central Station in Manhattan, then transferred to the nickel subway to Wall Street.

It was a far different Wall Street in the summer of 1932. There were no computers or split-second reports of stock trades. Everything was done on paper. From ticker tape, John W. and his co-workers entered stock price quotations on a large chalkboard and relayed trade prices to telegraph operators who passed along the information to Fenner and Beane offices around the country. The youthful floor workers also helped compute the Dow-Jones average.

John W. and his friends usually ate lunch at a Wall Street lunch counter where they took advantage of the "three hamburgers for a quarter" special. A soda cost a nickel.

The chance to work with veteran stock traders on Wall Street, the center of the world's business activity, was excellent training for the future businessman. The summer spent in New York City also heightened John's awareness of the ravages of the Great Depression. He remembered long soup lines that stretched around buildings on Wall Street.

John W. Nichols in October, 1936, while a student at the University of Oklahoma in Norman. During the Depression, his fraternity brothers and he were so short of cash that the staple of their diet was cabbage slaw.

two

....

Off to College

Going home to Ardmore was easy.
I walked out to US-77 and stuck out my thumb.

JOHN W. NICHOLS

The Great Depression had a stranglehold on Oklahoma and
the entire world when John arrived at the University
of Oklahoma in the fall of 1932. One of the reasons
he had chosen to attend OU was the low cost of tuition. The
affordability of the state-run university had become a factor
because low cotton prices reduced his father's income by at
least 50 percent.[1]

The Depression had begun in 1929 when the stock market crashed. It worsened as factories shut down, banks failed,
stores closed, and millions of Americans were left jobless and
homeless.

The suffering in Oklahoma was terrible. A searing drought
and the worst and longest economic downturn in history drove
people from the land in Oklahoma. Eventually, normally wet
Ardmore and Carter County were desiccated by the lack of
rainfall. In western Oklahoma, sand blew in such quantities
that travelers lost their way, chickens roosted at noon, airports

closed, and trains stopped. Animals and humans alike suffered from lung disorders.[2]

Oklahoma lost tens of thousands of people in the 1930s as they headed west to California. John Steinbeck immortalized the westward-bound Okies in *The Grapes of Wrath.* By 1932, more than one-fourth of the farmers in Oklahoma were on relief and nearly 20 percent of rural landowners were in default on land loans. Mortgage foreclosures were daily events.[3]

John was one of 5,000 students at OU in 1932. The university was established December 19, 1890, by act of the territorial legislature. It was located in Norman, the county seat of Cleveland County. When classes began at OU in 1892, enrollment was simple. Each student met with the president, Dr. David Ross Boyd, to obtain a printed schedule and then was examined by the faculty of four. The entire course listing was printed on one page.[4]

Dr. William Bennett Bizzell was president of OU in 1932. Bizzell had great faith in the university and brought OU to national prominence during the Great Depression. Many of the campus buildings were old and crowded. No student was allowed to have an automobile—any student discovered keeping a car somewhere in town was suspended.

John's father gave him a $1,000 check when he left for college. His instructions were simple—"Spend all of it quickly and have a big time, or keep it and make it last for the entire year." John heeded his father's advice and actually had $150 left at the end of his first year.

John was interested in the Delta Tau Delta fraternity at OU because several students from Ardmore were members. John arrived on campus early for Rush Week and pledged OU's Delta Alpha chapter of Delta Tau Delta.

The Delta Tau house had 40 members, making it one of the larger houses on campus. However, there was the problem of the $35-a-month cost of living in the Delta Tau House. Tuition and books were inexpensive, and his parents could provide that. But to help with additional expenses, John asked for and was given a job at the house waiting tables every other week. In return, he had to pay only $17.50, half the standard monthly room and board bill.

His work as a waiter caused him no loss of social standing in his fraternity, for the nation was gripped by the Depression. The reason he could only work every other week was because the fraternity wanted to spread the work around to help as many of its members as possible.

Delta Tau members slept on bunk beds in a large open room, although each member was assigned a roommate. John's first roommate was H.C. Luman of Oklahoma City.

John enjoyed his fraternity experience, surviving his freshman year with as much dignity as a pledge could muster. His initiation was a serious occasion, not one marked by hazing. Every Saturday night the pledges cleaned the Delt Shelter, as the Delta Tau House was called, under the watchful eye of Mother Allen, who had been the housemother since 1923.

Every Monday night in the Delta Shelter there was a chapter meeting, with no excuse for missing it. All in attendance had to wear a coat and tie. In addition, a coat and tie were mandatory at every Sunday lunch at the house. Attending class also involved more than casual dress. Delts were expected to wear slacks and a sport shirt in fall and spring. During the winter, on mild days, a sports coat was the norm, and on cold days a topcoat was added.

A natural leader, John was well liked by his fraternity brothers, and, following his pledge year, served the Delta Taus as social chairman, house manager, chairman of Rush Week activities, and delegate to the Intrafraternity Council. In addition, he was a member of Skeleton Key, Student Senate, and the Oratorical Council. In his senior year, he was elected president of the Delta Tau house.

John's loyalty to his fraternity has remained throughout his life. His Delta Tau Delta connection has benefited him greatly in business and in cementing life-long friendships. Later, as a successful businessman, John contributed to the construction of a new Delta Tau Delta house at OU, served as its chapter advisor, was president of the Western Division of the fraternity, and served as national president of Delta Tau Delta from 1962 until 1964.

John spent his freshman and sophomore years in general education classes—grammar, literature, history, government, math, science, philosophy, and introductory courses in business. When not in class or doing homework, he played intramural sports—touch football games in the fall and baseball in the spring. He played shortstop on the fraternity baseball team.

OU students paid a $5.00 activity fee that admitted them to all home sporting contests—football, basketball, baseball, and track meets—as well as cultural activities such as musical events and stage plays. Because a number of Delts were in the Jazz Hounds, a pep squad somewhat akin to the Roughnecks, John joined the group. They attended all home athletic contests to lead cheers and promote school spirit.

One member of John's pledge class, Bobby Shaw, made life dangerous for John. They were both enrolled in Army ROTC field artillery training, a compulsory class for male students at OU. Shaw said it was ridiculous that he and his close friends all had to attend Tuesday drill—so he devised a plan.[5]

Only one of four fraternity brothers would show up at the weekly drill. However, when his other friends' names were called, he yelled "Here, sir!" For a while, the plan worked beautifully. Then, one day, the ROTC commandant, caught on to the trick and requested that John accompany him to the armory.[6]

Major Maloney threatened to report John's action of answering roll call for his fraternity brothers unless John would name his co-conspirators. John refused and took a great chance that the commandant would give him 100 demerits and cause him to fail the mandatory course. However, the officer saddled John with only 99 demerits and demanded that he work them off—one hour for one demerit—at the ROTC stables which housed horses that pulled the French 75-mm cannon, a World War I remnant, used by the OU field artillery unit. John shoveled out the stables for what seemed like months until he erased the demerits from his record.[7]

The social life for fraternity and sorority members at OU revolved around dances. Each house had a social chairman and the Intrafraternity Council coordinated social activities. Generally, some fraternity arranged a dance every week except the week before final examinations. Several times a year formal dances were scheduled. Each fraternity sent stag invitations to other fraternities to increase the pool of men at dances. College men were expected to own a tuxedo and be comfortable wearing it. College women were expected to own an evening gown.

Because girls in sororities had an early curfew, money was scarce, and there were no automobiles, a date usually meant walking off campus to a drug store for a soft drink. Five dollars went a long way. John remembered, "Going downtown to a movie could be a major expense at 25 cents each and the cost of refreshments. Or, if the young man really wanted to impress a date, he could take her downtown by taxi, which also cost 25 cents."[8]

During his freshman year, John established the habit of going home to Ardmore to visit his parents at least once in the fall, at Thanksgiving, and during the Christmas recess. To get to Ardmore was simple. On Friday afternoon he walked east of the OU campus to US-77 and stuck out his thumb. In no time at all, some generous motorist would give him a ride, if not all the way to Ardmore, then at least to Pauls Valley. Then someone else would pick him up and take him farther south until he arrived in Ardmore. On Sunday afternoon the process was reversed as he hitchhiked back to Norman.

During John's sophomore year, 1933-1934, his father accepted a position with Fenner and Beane. With the new job came a move to Oklahoma City in the spring of 1934, where John's parents rented an apartment at the intersection of Northwest 22nd Street and Walker Avenue. Afterward, John simply rode the interurban to Oklahoma City for family visits.

John enrolled in mostly accounting and business courses for his junior year at OU. A professor who made a lasting impression on him was Dr. Arthur Adams, Dean of the College of Business Administration. John took four courses from Dean Adams in his final two years of college. Another professor who was a favorite of John's was W.K. Newton, head of the accounting department.[9]

After spending the summer of 1935 chauffeuring Aunt Lillian around California, John returned for his senior year with the idea that he needed his own car for transportation. He and another Delt found a way to get around the university's ban on students owning cars. They bought a new Ford and registered it in the name of the other boy's cousin who had a different last name and lived in Maysville, Oklahoma. John was cautious to not overuse the automobile, especially on dates.

Mary Davis graduated from McAlester High
School in 1933 as valedictorian of her class.

three

....

Along Came Mary

*I tagged Mary by mistake, but it was the
luckiest moment of my life.*

JOHN W. NICHOLS

T he years have faded the story of how John met his future
wife, Mary, in 1936. Both have a different account—
but one part of the story is common—their first date
was accidental—or at least, fateful.

It was during a dance in April, 1936, that John and Mary
Davis spoke to each other for the first time. He was a senior—
she was a junior. She was a popular girl who was often invited
to dances at John's fraternity house. Mary was social chairman
of the Kappa Kappa Gamma sorority. She and John recognized
each other but had never had a conversation.

Mary was at the fateful night's dance with Sigma Alpha
Epsilon member Bill Barnes, who had been invited to the event
by John.

During a "tag" dance, John moved onto the dance floor with
the intent of dancing with Mary Trapp, a Theta. He walked up
behind who he thought was Mary Trapp and tapped her escort's

arm, expecting him to step aside. Much to John's surprise, the girl was not Mary Trapp—it was Mary Davis. The mistake was honest because the two Marys looked very much alike.

As John was trying to explain his mistake, a bell rang. It was customary for couples dancing together at the time the bell rang to stay together during a short intermission. John and Mary had a Coca-Cola and enjoyed each other's company very much. It was the first of a dozen dates during John's last two months as a student at OU.[1]

Mary's parents lived in McAlester, Oklahoma, where her father, Dr. James Edward Davis, was a prominent physician. Born in Greenback, Tennessee, and raised in Morgantown, Tennessee, Dr. Davis graduated from the University of Tennessee and then Hospital Medical School at Louisville, Kentucky, to earn his M.D. degree. He completed his specialty training in Philadelphia, Pennsylvania, and his internship, residency, and advanced training as a specialist in the area of eye, ear, nose, and throat in New York, New York.

While in New York City he met and fell in love with Mary Bailey, originally from Temple, Texas, where her father, Jesse Luther Bailey, owned a large number of farms in the area known as the Blackland Prairie. Mary, known as "Byrdie" because of her beautiful singing voice, graduated from Temple High School and then nearby Baylor Female Institute, now Mary Hardin-Baylor University. After graduation, she traveled to New York City to visit her sister who was married to a Texas physician. After a "very proper" courtship, Byrdie and Dr. Davis were married and set up an apartment in New York City while he completed his residency.[2]

In 1910, with Dr. Davis' residency and advanced training complete and Byrdie several months along with her first pregnancy, they decided to visit her family in Temple. The trip

Mary "Byrdie" Davis and
five-month-old Mary Davis.

Mary Davis grew up in a loving home in McAlester.

was planned to allow them to visit several communities where Dr. Davis might establish his medical practice. Traveling on the Katy Railroad into Oklahoma, Byrdie became ill and they decided to stop in McAlester to allow her time to recover. Some time later, they chose McAlester as their new home.

McAlester traced its history to 1869 when it began as a spot of wilderness in southeastern Indian Territory where the Texas Road, the wagon trail from Missouri to Texas, crossed a California trail running from Fort Smith, Arkansas, to the West Coast. The town was named for prominent business-man, J.J. McAlester, who built the first tent store at the crossroads and was later Oklahoma's second lieutenant governor. McAlester was the county seat of Pittsburg County that took its name from Pittsburgh, Pennsylvania, home to many of the coal miners who came to work mines in southeast Oklahoma after the Civil War.[3]

Soon after establishing his practice, the couple's first child, Addie Lee, was born. Five years later, in 1916, another daughter arrived—this one named Mary, after her mother. Later two more children arrived to complete the household—a third daughter, Mildred, and a son, James Edward.

Mary had a wonderful childhood. Her best friend was Helen McCarley, the daughter of another local physician. The two girls were inseparable and even formed their own "sorority," PDK, which stood for "Playing Dolls Club." A local jeweler made them sorority pins emblazoned with the Greek letters, PDK.

Mary's parents were active in McAlester's First Presbyterian Church. Her mother taught Sunday school, sang in the choir, and wrote articles for religious magazines. Mary's parents were brilliant scholars and were very interested in her education. Her father's strong points were math and science—he always made time to help her with complicated homework. Mary's mother had a degree in English and music and gave Mary a love for the arts and literature.

In summers, Mary attended performances of William Shakespeare's works. She took piano lessons for a while, but turned to playing the flute for the high school band and orchestra. While her mother encouraged growth in the arts, Mary's father helped with science and math homework. Mary remembered, "I had the best of both worlds. I was blessed with very intelligent parents whose talents complimented each other and were distributed to their offspring for generations."[4]

Mary Davis on the steps of the Kappa Kappa Gamma house at the University of Oklahoma in 1937.

After high school, Mary and Helen McCarley decided to attend Randolph-Macon Woman's College in Lynchburg, Virginia. After a three-day train trip from McAlester to Randolph-Macon, Mary and Helen were disappointed to discover they would not be allowed to room together. However, they managed to be assigned dormitory rooms across the hall from each other. Mary remained at Randolph-Macon through her freshman year and then decided to enroll at the University of Oklahoma.

Mary came to Norman for Rush Week in September of 1934 and pledged Kappa Kappa Gamma. A popular young lady, Mary's social life was full. She refused to date any boy "steady."

Instead, she had casual dates with a number of boys, sometimes three in a single day and evening. Most dates involved meeting at the Student Union Building on campus or at one of the corner drug stores just off campus.

She enjoyed sorority life at OU. When she and other sisters sat down for dinner, it was with a tablecloth, china, and silverware. Boys wearing white jackets waited on

Mary Davis graduated Phi Beta Kappa from the University of Oklahoma. This photograph was taken in October, 1936.

them. The girls were close because they were together most of the time. Sorority members were not allowed to have a car on campus and the Great Depression had limited extra money for entertainment. The girls were under a strict curfew—10:30 p.m. on weeknights and midnight on Friday and Saturday nights.[5]

With money scarce, the girls often pooled their change to pay a quarter for a taxi ride to the Sooner Theater on Main Street in Norman. They saved an extra quarter fare by asking the driver to let them off just west of the railroad tracks near the theater. The tracks separated taxi zones—going the extra few feet doubled the fare.

Mary went to all home football games, a requirement of her sorority during her pledge year. She was fortunate to date a young man who was an authority on football and took the time to teach the game to her. She has been an avid OU football fan since that time.

Mary was an excellent student and as a sophomore was named to the honor plaque and was elected to Mortar Board. During her junior year, her fellow class members chose her class vice president. In addition, her sorority sisters chose her to be their social chairman. She graduated Phi Beta Kappa in 1937 with a degree in arts and sciences.

John closed out his senior year as president of the Delta Tau house. The campus newspaper lauded his achievements in a story under the headline, "Chapter Has Fine Year Under Nichols." The reporter suggested that John's approaching graduation would leave a "lamentable gap" in leadership of the fraternity.

Even though John gave credit to the other members of the fraternity, he was proud of the Delta Tau accomplishments. The fraternity was first in scholarship among all OU fraternities for the third consecutive semester, was first in the intrafraternity sing, and ranked high in intramural athletic competition. A crowning achievement was the fraternity placing number one nationally in the 1936 fraternity examination given new members.[6]

Early in June,1936, John graduated from OU with a Bachelor of Science degree in business. Before he began working a steady job, however, he—along with three friends also finishing their degrees—wanted one last summer of carefree adventure.

John W. Nichols and a lady friend on an English beach during the 1936 trip to Europe. Nichols and his Oklahoma friends could not believe their good fortune of hosting young ladies on tour in exchange for room and board.

four
....

Gigolo in Paris

*We never dreamed we could earn room and board
just by dating pretty young girls every night.*

JOHN W. NICHOLS

fter commencement in June, 1936, John teamed up with
good friends, Beauchamp Selmon, Charles "Chub"
Bell, and E.L. Evans, for the trip of a lifetime. They had
their entire trip planned well because their Delta Tau fraternity
brother, Bobby Shaw, had lived in Barcelona, Spain, before coming to America for college. Shaw was scheduled to meet John
and his friends in Barcelona when they arrived. Shaw spoke
fluent Spanish and would be the tour guide as the five recently
graduated OU students saw the sights of Spain and the rest of
Europe.

On July 1, 1936, John, Selmon, Bell, and Evans arrived in
Galveston, Texas, where they had booked passage to Europe
on a freighter owned by the Lykes Steamship Company, a
firm that shipped cotton from America to spinning mills in
Barcelona. Paying $54.25 each, John and his friends boarded
the S.S. *Syros* for the voyage across the Atlantic. They each

The official photograph in John's passport issued for the 1936 trip to Europe.

carried $500 cash, hopefully sufficient money to stay in Europe for two months.

John's diary is filled with details of the trip across the choppy ocean. There was not a great deal to do on the freighter except read, play checkers, cards, and other board games, and partake of the excellent food on board. Soup was served for lunch and a full course dinner was available each evening. On June 30, John wrote in his diary, "Got up at 7:30, laid in sun and got sunburned until 11:00…ate lunch and played monopoly…then took a shower and cleaned. Ate dinner and then played more monopoly."[1]

Chub Bell, later an Oklahoma City drilling contractor, spent much of his time writing home. Beachamp Selmon was John's best friend. He later was best man when John married Mary Davis and was a successful insurance broker in Tulsa. The fourth member of the Sooner band crossing the sea was E.L. Evans, who after college became a banker and rancher in Ardmore.

By July 4, 1936, the *Syros* moved out of the Gulf of Mexico and into the Atlantic Ocean. John recorded the passing in his diary, "About 6:00 we passed Miami [Florida] where we could see the tall buildings. After dinner we could see the lights of Palm Beach [Florida] and also the fireworks. Watched the moon come up and thought of home."[2]

The boredom of the 26-day trip across the ocean was evidenced by John's daily entry in his diary. On July 16, noting heaving swells and cold and cloudy conditions, John recorded the fact that he and Chub were tied at 41 games each in checkers—and they had only been keeping score for three days.[3]

Left to right, Charles "Chub" Bell, E.L. Evans, and John W. Nichols were three of the four OU students who spent much of the summer of 1936 in Europe. The fourth member of the traveling group was Beauchamp Selmon.

On July 19, the *Syros* sailed through the Straits of Gibraltar. John wrote that the Mediterranean Sea was "smooth as a mill pond and very blue."[4] He and his friends were disturbed when the ship's radio operator relayed information about revolutionary fighting in Spain—the Spanish Civil War had erupted while they were on the high seas.

John was counting on Bobby Shaw to lead the travels across Europe. However, when the *Syros* sailed into Barcelona on July 21 and dropped anchor, they discovered that Shaw and his family had returned to America when the fighting had started. Nearly half of Barcelona was in flames.

It was too dangerous for the freighter to dock, so to avoid being bombed, the captain of the *Syros* ordered the vessel to a small coastal village named Tarragona, where the cotton bales had to be offloaded by hand.

Although John and the others were told not to get off the ship, they decided to go ashore where they saw rebels burning churches and shooting their guns into the air. John recorded the sights, "There were men riding around in cars with signs painted on them and holding up their fists."[5] John climbed over a line of sandbags and saw machine guns everywhere. He remembered, "It's a wonder we didn't get shot!"[6]

The next day Tarragona's harbor was bombed. The four Americans were offered evacuation on a British destroyer that was leaving port within hours. But, all four chose to stay, boarding the *Syros* a few days later when it sailed for Genoa, Italy.

After arriving in Genoa, Italy. They obtained additional money from the local American Express office. Nichols and his three friends saw the local sites, and then traveled by train to Milan and on to Venice, enjoying the canals of that ancient city in a gondola.

The Brandenburg Gate in Berlin, Germany, during the Olympic games in 1936. German flags emblazoned with swastikas hung from the gate alongside the official Olympic flag.

John and his three Oklahoma friends toured Berlin in August, 1936, in an open tourmobile. John has his hand on his chin toward the rear of the vehicle.

From Italy they made their way north to Switzerland and then to Berlin, Germany, which was hosting the 1936 Olympic games. At the Berlin American Express office, John received two letters from Mary, his first word from home. The

American Express office was also a great source of information about American girls touring Berlin. Each night, John and his friends tried to make their paths cross the paths of the girls' tours.

The boys attended the opening ceremonies of the Olympics in Berlin's Olympic Stadium. German Chancellor Adolf Hitler, who had been in power three years and was preparing his people for an attempted conquest of Europe and the entire world, presided over the opening of the Olympics. John remembered the German soldiers being very friendly but "full of Hitler's propaganda." In John's opinion, "the brainwashing had begun."[7]

After Berlin, John and the others traveled by train to Paris, France, the City of Lights. They were running low on money and looked for some way to work out their room and board in Paris.

John snapped this photograph as he entered New York harbor on his return to the United States in 1936. The Empire State Building tops the horizon. To its right is the Chrysler Building, under construction at the time.

What they found was a tour company that would provide them a place to stay and their meals in exchange for the young men serving as escorts for young women who were on tour in Paris. All John and his cohorts had to do was to wear their tuxedos, that had been gingerly packed in one of two suitcases each boy carried on the trip, and show up well-groomed for the evening tour. They called themselves "the gigolos from Oklahoma."

From Paris the four young men took a train to Amsterdam and Rotterdam, Holland, and Brussels, Belgium, before arriving in England, where John's Aunt Lillian was staying at the

Savoy Hotel in London. By then, the young travelers were out of money. Aunt Lillian financed their sightseeing tour of England and bought them third-class tickets home aboard the S.S. *Aquitania*, a passenger ship owned by the Cunard White Star Line.

John, back row right, and Beauchamp Selmon, back row left, pose with three of the young ladies they escorted in exchange for room and board in Paris, France, in 1936.

The boys only ate in third class, but when the cocktail hour started, they put on their tuxedos and made their way to the first-class area of the ship. There were guards to keep the classes separated, but seeing John and the others in tuxedos, the guards thought they were first-class passengers and allowed them admission. On deck, John saw one girl from Oklahoma City and another young lady from OU. The return trip from Europe—7 days—was much shorter than the 26-day journey aboard the freighter two months earlier.

The sojourn to Europe ended when the *Aquitania* docked in New York City on September 2, 1936, where one of John's cousins, Carl Whiteman, was president of General Foods. After showing them the sights, he put them on a train for the three-day ride back to Oklahoma.

This photograph in the McAlester newspaper announced Mary and John's wedding on August 28, 1937. It is the only photograph that remains of their wedding. The photographer hired for the occasion did such a poor job that all photographs were thrown away.

five
....

Courtship
and Marriage

I love you with so much of my heart,
there is none left to protest.

WILLIAM SHAKESPEARE

J ohn *was 22, had a college degree*—but no job—when he
returned to Oklahoma City in the fall of 1936. Bob Rapp,
a friend of his father's, suggested that John contact Otto
Thompson of the Denver Producing and Refining Company
who was looking for a bookkeeper. Headquartered in Oklahoma
City, the firm operated a number of oil and natural gas wells on
behalf of royalty owners. Impressed with John, Thompson
hired him at a salary of $125 a month, which soon was cut to
$100 per month because of the economic downturn. John's
main duty was to handle the firm's payroll.

By this time John's parents had moved into a home at
1204 Northwest 40th Street in the Crown Heights section
of Oklahoma City, and he was living with them. However,
$100 a month did not go all that far for a young man driving

to Norman several evenings a week in his parents' car to court Mary Davis, who was in her senior year at OU. John and Mary had exchanged a few letters over the summer.

John had not realized that while he was in Europe, a young man whom Mary knew from OU had courted her. In fact, the youth spent the summer in McAlester with a fraternity brother just to be close to Mary. Finally, Mary was so tired of him, she told the family maid, "I don't want to see him. When he calls, tell him I've gone to town."[1] That eliminated John's only serious rival for Mary's affection.

John and Mary's dates took them to football games when the Sooners played at home and to fraternity dances on Saturday nights. With John having a car, they could easily drive downtown to a movie. But many nights they simply walked from Mary's sorority house to a local drug store, where they would sit at the soda fountain and drink Coca-Cola while talking the endless talk of young people who were falling in love.

On December 20, 1936, during Mary's senior year, her parents were killed, and her sister Mildred injured, in an automobile accident near Shawnee, Oklahoma. Mary's older sister, Addie Lee, just two years out of college, had to become mother to Mildred who was injured so badly she could not continue classes in her senior year of high school. Mary remembered, "I don't know how we made it without parents, losing them so early in life. But mother and daddy had trained us well and

Dr. James Edward Davis, the father of Mary Davis Nichols. Dr. Davis was born May 17, 1879, and was killed along with his wife in an automobile accident just before Christmas in 1936. After their untimely deaths, Samuel R. Braden, pastor of McAlester's First Presbyterian Church said, "They are so closely identified with spiritual-mindedness and righteousness in this community that we owe them our deepest consideration." The McAlester newspaper called Dr. Davis' death "a distinct community loss which has left a big vacancy."

Mary "Byrdie" Davis' last act was decorating a Christmas tree for her Sunday School class at First Presbyterian Church in McAlester shortly before she and her husband were killed in an accident in 1936.

had equipped us with the moral standards to make it on our own."[2]

Fortunately, the estate left by her parents allowed Mary and her siblings to complete their college education. John was a source of strength for Mary during this period, and on New Year's Eve, 1936, he proposed. The wedding was scheduled for August 28, 1937.

John and Mary were married in McAlester's First Presbyterian Church on Saturday afternoon, August 28, 1937, with her sister, Addie Lee Milner, serving as matron of honor, and her other sister, Mildred, as maid of honor. Helen McCarley, Frances Myers, Bettie Hayden, and Rosa Lee Lewis were bridesmaids. John's

John and the men of Mary's family. Left to right, Wayne Milner, married to Mary's sister, Addie Lee; John; Mary's brother, Jim Davis; and Charles Richard, the husband of Mary's other sister, Mildred.

best man was Beauchamp Selmon. His ushers were Richard Yeager, Joe Fred Gibson, Rhys Evans, William Whiteman, and H.C. Luman.

John's Aunt Lillian Simpson gave the couple a new 1937 Dodge as a wedding present. They headed for Eureka Springs, Arkansas, and then on to Branson and St. Louis, Missouri, and finally the Peabody Hotel in Memphis, Tennessee, for their honeymoon. After spending their last night dancing to Bob Crosby and his orchestra at the Peabody, they departed the next morning for McAlester and Oklahoma City.

Unfortunately, they had over spent their budget. John looked in the pockets of his suit but did not find a penny. Mary's purse was also empty. When they stopped at a store in the Ouachita Mountains, another customer dropped a dime in the dirt. Mary moved quickly to stand over the dime. When the man gave up his search for the lost dime, Mary used the coin to purchase a box of popcorn for lunch, causing John to remark, "Oh no, I've married a thief."[3]

The gasoline that remained in their car got them to Wilburton, Oklahoma, about 30 miles east of McAlester. John pulled into a service station at nightfall, explained they that were on their way to McAlester, and asked to write a 15-cent check for one gallon of gasoline. The attendant said, "No."

Mary intervened and explained that her father had been a physician in McAlester, and that her check was good. The attendant recognized Dr. Davis as the physician who had removed his children's tonsils and allowed Mary to write a check for a dollar for gasoline. However, the attendant would not accept a check for enough money for a single hamburger for the honeymooners. Mary wondered, "Have I chosen the right man?" She later told John she thought she had married someone who could support her.[4]

Arriving in Oklahoma City, the newlyweds rented a $35-per-month duplex at 409 Northwest 32nd Street. By this time John was making $125 a month and Mary received $100 a month from her parents' insurance policy. Their social life revolved around such friends as Howard and Mearl Melton, John and Mary Lou Carnahan, Lois and Chuck Stewart, and Bernard and Betty Kennedy. In addition to playing card games and attending movies, John and Mary joined several dance clubs.

In 1939, T. Dwight Williams, who, along with Ford Billups, owned T. Dwight Williams Accounting, approached John. Williams, who had met John while his accounting firm was auditing Denver Producing and Refining Company, offered him a salary of $175 a month to move to his firm. However, to qualify for the job, John first had to pass the examination required to become a certified public accountant (CPA). He was successful and was given certificate number 460, making him the 460th person to become a CPA in Oklahoma history. In 2004, the newest CPA in the state was assigned number 15,636.

Specializing in auditing oil companies, the T. Dwight Williams offices were located in downtown Oklahoma City where John regularly came into contact with many independent oilmen. As the junior member of the accounting firm, John often was assigned tasks that were the least profitable for the firm. One of John's clients was the Oklahoma City Golf and Country Club, which he joined in 1943 for dues of $10 per month and no initiation fee. John was able to join the exclusive country club only because he was auditing the books and became aware that a club member had died. Because of the rule that allowed the purchase of a membership from a deceased member's estate without a transfer fee, John was allowed to join the country club for $125. Forty years later, a membership cost more than $20,000.[5]

An increase in salary allowed John and Mary to build a four-bedroom, two-bath home in 1939 at 1715 Pennington Way in the Nichols Hills area. Its total cost was $12,500. The Nichols lived there until 1963. *Courtesy Mattison Avenue Publishing Company.*

When World War II broke out on December 7, 1941, John rushed to enlist in the Navy, believing it was his patriotic duty. However, he was rejected because of his flat feet. A year later, in 1942, he was drafted. At the induction center he was asked about the arm he had broken as a child. The examining orthopedic surgeon ordered John to the Medical Arts Building for an x-ray. After viewing the first x-ray, the physician ordered him to St. Anthony Hospital for a second one. This time John was accompanied by a sergeant who was ordered to hand carry the x-ray back to the induction center. After examining the new film, the doctor released John from military service because his arm had not healed properly. John then attempted to serve his country by joining the Federal Bureau of Investigation. Again he was rejected because of medical reasons.

Like all other Americans, John and Mary endured the shortages and rationing of World War II. Fortunately they were able to supplement their meat ration by acquiring beef from a friend who owned a ranch. This helped, because John and Mary had two children before the war ended, and they faced a constant struggle to feed four people on their ration stamps.

Their first child, John Larry Nichols, was born on July 6, 1942. A daughter, Betty Ann Nichols, arrived on November 23, 1944, and a second son, James Kent Nichols, was born on October 5, 1949.

Wartime rationing also limited individuals to two pairs of shoes a year. Also, only the most popular sizes were manufactured—a problem for Mary who had small feet. She simply could not find shoes to fit. To solve the problem, she bought larger sizes and put cardboard in them to keep them on.

Because his work at an auditing firm required travel and was considered essential to the war effort, John was able to get extra gasoline ration stamps. However, to conserve gasoline, the federal government had passed legislation limiting the speed limit nationally to just 35 miles an hour, and, of course, there were no freeways at that time. The 100-mile drive to Tulsa usually took at least four hours.

F.G. "Blackie" Blackwood was John Nichols' first partner in the oil business. John described Blackie as "the perfect partner." *Courtesy Charles Blackwood.*

six

Blackwood & Nichols

*The more I learned about the oil business,
the more fascinated I became.*

JOHN W. NICHOLS

Among the independent oil operators in the same building
with the T. Dwight Williams' Accounting Firm was
F. G. "Blackie" Blackwood, a burly, likeable six-footer
who looked like a fullback on a college football team. Blackie
was 13 years older than John and had developed his physique
in the oil patch bucking long sections of drill pipe for the
Indian Territory Illuminating Oil Company (ITIO), first on
cable tool rigs and then on rotary platforms. As a result he
knew the oil business from the ground up.

Because Blackie wanted to be more than a roughneck or
tool pusher, he leased a small piece of land in the Oklahoma
City Field. There were no spacing regulations at the time and,
on the tiny spot of ground, Blackie drilled a well that eventually produced more than one million barrels of oil. With that

start, he moved on to buying and selling leases and drilling an occasional well, usually with partners.

The more John learned about the oil business, the more fascinated he became. Realizing that he would never become wealthy on his salary as a CPA, he was interested when Blackie came to him in 1941 with an opportunity to buy into an oil deal.

Blackie and his wife, Dola; E.C. Loosen of Okarche, Oklahoma, and his wife, Kathleen; and Genevieve Williams, the wife of CPA Dwight Williams, needed only a few thousand dollars more to fund a royalty interest purchase in the Keystone Field in the Permian Basin of Winkler County, Texas.[1]

It was a big gamble for John who, in February, 1941, paid $6,250 for 20 percent of the royalty available in the sale. The purchase price was equal to John and Mary's total savings, but after discussing it, both decided that the potential outweighed the risk.[2]

Although it proved to be a wise decision, several months passed before the success of the investment became apparent. John's first monthly check was $19, causing Mary to question John's ability as an oil and gas entrepreneur. However, World War II began shortly thereafter and drilling and royalty checks increased. As the larger checks rolled into the Nichols household, Mary thought John was a hero. In 2003, 62 years later, the Nichols received an average of $3,612 monthly from the $6,250 investment.

John occasionally invested in oil and gas properties over the next few years, especially with the help of a college friend, William "Bill" Hilseweck, who married Helen McCarley, Mary's closest friend from McAlester. Bill graduated as the top OU geology student and was working as a geologist for Gulf Oil Company in Midland, the center of activity in the Permian Basin in West Texas.

From time to time, Bill told John where oil companies were planning to drill new wells. Blackie then would quickly purchase mineral interests near the wildcat, while John worked hard to sell three-quarters of the lease for 100 percent of the cost.[3]

The development of the Dollarhide Field in Texas is an example of how John hit the big time in oil and gas production. In early, 1945, Bill called John with a tip that the Pure Oil Company was about to drill in a field in far west Texas, Andrews County, along the Texas-New Mexico border.

The barren ranchland was part of the famous XIT Ranch, given to an English company in exchange for construction of a new Texas State Capitol in Austin from 1885 to 1888. The XIT was once the world's largest ranch, covering three million acres in 10 counties in West Texas. The ranch was twice the size of Rhode Island.[4]

The XIT ranch supposedly had 6,000 miles of fence at one time. A 175-mile long fence was built on what was recognized as the Texas-New Mexico state line on the southwest side of the ranch. When years later it was discovered the fence was 400 yards off the actual boundary, Congress changed the states' boundary to prevent moving the long stretch of fence.

John discovered that one of the major mineral owners in the Dollarhide Field, Sam Gloyd, lived in Oklahoma City. He went to Gloyd's office in the First National Bank Building and met with Gloyd's office manager. John was told that Gloyd owned one-eighth mineral interest in a quarter section of six sections of land in the field. Gloyd's manager informed John that his boss never sold mineral interests but would be interested in leasing the land for $50 an acre and one-eighth royalty on any production.[5]

John was thrilled and prepared the lease for Gloyd's signature. However, when he showed up at Gloyd's office to get the lease signed, Gloyd said he would only make the deal if John leased 25 sections of land in the region, a far greater investment than John could make. John told Gloyd about his agreement with the office manager. Gloyd turned to the manager and said, "Is Nichols right?" When the manager confirmed what he had promised John, Gloyd signed the lease on May 16, 1945, and lived up to the deal made by his employee. "That kind of honesty and fair dealing would not have occurred decades later in the oil and gas business," John said.[6]

What seemed like a good deal for John and Blackie initially went sour. Every time Pure Oil Company drilled a well on the lease, Blackwood & Nichols had to pay one-eighth of the drilling costs. Blackie was concerned that the leases in the Dollarhide Field would soon break them. Some days John thought that he and Blackie owed more money to their principal financier, Republic National Bank of Dallas, than they would ever be worth.[7]

However, caverns of oil were found underneath the West Texas plains. Eventually, more than 100 wells were drilled in the field, many of them to double and triple layers of sand. In 2003, John received an average of $7,936 monthly from the $2,700 investment in 1945.[8]

In early 1946, Blackie suggested to John one Wednesday afternoon that they use gasoline ration stamps and drive to Midland, Texas, to scout the region for prospective oil investments. John agreed and asked Ford Billups for two days off work. Billups agreed. But when John returned to work, Dwight Williams confronted him for being absent. John got angry and quit. When he got home and told Mary what had happened, she said, "My gosh! What are we going to do?" John told her, "I don't know, but I've quit."[9]

John decided to join Blackie in oil and gas investments fulltime. They began their partnership with a handshake. They did not incorporate or even form an official partnership—they simply invested jointly in whatever properties caught their attention. Blackie spotted the potential investments and John kept the books in their tiny office. John remembered, "Blackie and I would hustle around to wherever things looked promising."[10]

Mineral interests were cheap, often $25 an acre. Wherever there was an oil play, John and Blackie paid for interests with a 30-day draft. They quickly sold 75 percent of the interest for what they had paid for the entire interest. With what they received for selling, they covered their draft and had a quarter interest left to divide.[11]

Because of his training as a CPA, John understood the tax advantages of investing in the oil and gas business. There was tax-free income on 27.5 percent of gross income. Also, intangible drilling costs were allowed to be deducted in the year which they were incurred and there was no alternative minimum federal income tax.

During World War II, the income tax rate for Americans in the highest income brackets soared to 90 percent. These wealthy individuals depended on income from invested capital. But after taxes, most of them had to dip into their principal for sufficient income to meet living expenses. John's task was to convince these people that an investment in the oil business was the solution to their problem.

Because nearly nine of every ten wildcat wells produced nothing but dust, during the war years the federal government assumed much of the risk for wildcat drilling. If the hole was dry, its entire cost—including labor, fuel, trucking, tools, and consumable materials—was deductible from the individual's taxable income from all sources. As John explained to potential investors, the federal government paid 90 percent of the cost of a dry hole.

However, if oil was found, the government still paid about 60 percent of a well's cost because the investor could deduct intangible drilling costs from his taxable income that year. In addition, there was the depletion allowance on production.

Producing oil or gas obviously depleted reserves still in the ground—therefore, the government allowed an investor to consider 27.5 percent of gross income as return on capital. Taxes were due only on the remaining 72.5 percent of the income after deducting drilling and production costs and depreciation on tangible equipment.[12]

While still a CPA for T. Dwight Williams Accounting, John had begun to study the tax laws and how they could be used to accumulate wealth. He audited Amerada Petroleum in Tulsa and Kerr-Lynn Oil Company, predecessor of Kerr-McGee Corporation, in Oklahoma City. He saw how the companies used intangible drilling costs, the depletion allowance, and depreciation of assets to both lower its tax bills as well as increase the buying power of its drilling dollars. John rationalized that if it was prudent for a corporation to do that, then why would it not be even more advantageous for an individual in the 90 percent tax bracket?

John was getting a free education in complicated tax and oil investment laws. He began using his knowledge of the tax advantages of investing in oil as he sold interests in his and Blackie's leases. Initially, most of his sales were to friends and acquaintances with limited investment income.

Soon John realized that more investment money was needed and suggested that he and Blackie form a partnership that would appeal to large income investors. The perfect opportunity to put this plan into effect came during the summer of 1946, and it, like so many other opportunities in John's life, grew out of his years at the University of Oklahoma.

The end of wartime rationing revived the production of commercial goods and created a great demand for gasoline, leading to an almost unprecedented level of activity in the oil industry as investors flocked to the oil patch. Tragically, the business was cursed with men selling shares in phony drilling schemes that hurt honest promoters such as John and Blackie, who had built a solid and honest reputation.

In the summer of 1946, John, Mary, their two children, and their maid, Gladys Sparks, decided to vacation in the woods of Minnesota. Unfortunately, the woods greatly aggravated Mary's allergies. To escape the pollen, John and Mary left their children in the maid's care and traveled to Chicago, Illinois, to attend the first Delta Tau Delta national convention to be held after the end of World War II. It was staged in the historic Palmer House and John and Mary looked forward to renewing old friendships.

Also attending the convention was John W. Fisher of Tennessee, whom John had first met in 1936 at the Southern regional meeting of the fraternity. A Tennessee native, Fisher had enrolled at the University of Tennessee on an athletic scholarship in 1934 and became a member of Delta Tau Delta. He graduated in 1938 with a bachelor of science degree in factory management.

After graduation, Fisher spent the next two years serving as field secretary of the Delta Taus, and then in the fall of 1940 enrolled in the Harvard School of Business Administration. He had met, courted, and in August of 1940, married Janice Ball of Muncie, Indiana. Her father was one of five brothers who had founded the Ball Glass Company. In addition to making glass jars, the company had holdings in zinc, rubber, and paper manufacturing, all essential to the war effort.

Fisher eventually took an active role in management of Ball Glass, including looking after the company's oil properties in the southwestern United States.

It was Fisher's experience with the oil properties that made him aware of the tax advantages of investing in drilling for oil and gas. When he came to the Delta Tau Delta convention in Chicago in 1946, he hoped to meet a fraternity brother who would help him invest Ball family money in petroleum ventures.

In Chicago, Fisher learned that John was at the convention and that he dealt in oil and natural gas investments. Each seemed to be the answer to the other's needs. Blackwood & Nichols had a track record of conservative investment in oil leases and production that generated a steady return without unnecessary risk. Fisher wanted to invest his own money and the Ball family fortune in a way that would allow them to keep more than a scant 10 percent.

John, Blackie, and Fisher organized an informal partnership. Thanks to a prudent and conservative investment approach, there were handsome dividends from the producing leases in which they purchased royalty interests. They often used a few thousand dollars of capital to generate "a small fortune." They also participated in many farm-outs and deals that added to their reputation for honesty, reliability, and conservatism within the oil patch.[13]

PROSPECTUS

$3,500,000 Contributions in
Oil Property Interests

Blackwood & Nichols Company
and
Davidson, Hartz, Hyde & Dewey, Inc.

THESE SECURITIES HAVE NOT BEEN APPROVED OR DISAPPROVED BY
THE SECURITIES AND EXCHANGE COMMISSION NOR HAS THE
COMMISSION PASSED UPON THE ACCURACY OR ADEQUACY
OF THIS PROSPECTUS. ANY REPRESENTATION TO
THE CONTRARY IS A CRIMINAL OFFENSE.

	Price to Public	Underwriting Discounts	Net Cash Proceeds
Total	(See text below)	(See text below)	(See text below)
Per Unit	(See text below)	(See text below)	(See text below)

Solicitations for contributions will be made by Davidson, Hartz, Hyde & Dewey, Inc. No contributions will be accepted in an amount less than $5,000, although contributions in excess of $5,000 need not be in multiples thereof. The full amount of contributions received will be held for the benefit of Contributors and there will be no underwriting discounts or commissions in the ordinary sense. Blackwood & Nichols Company will be paid the sum of $500 per month for each exploratory well and each initial proven acreage farm-out well beginning on the date when drilling on any such well is commenced and terminating when it is plugged or becomes subject to an operating agreement with the Contributors. Also, Davidson, Hartz, Hyde & Dewey, Inc. will be allowed a maximum of 1% of contributions actually received for the purpose of defraying such expenses as rendering reports and other pertinent information to Contributors. The acquisition costs of unproven acreage and the costs of drilling and completing the exploratory well thereon will be paid solely out of contributions. It is anticipated that not more than 75% of the contributions will be used for this class of expenditure. As to all other types of property, the costs of acquisition, exploration, development and operation, both as to working and non-working interests, will be paid in the ratio of 75% by the Contributors and 25% by Blackwood & Nichols Company and Davidson, Hartz, Hyde & Dewey, Inc. All interest in oil property however acquired will be owned in the ratio of 62½% by Contributors, in individual interests according to their respective contributions, and 37½% by Blackwood & Nichols Company and Davidson, Hartz, Hyde & Dewey, Inc. according to the agreement between them. An exception to the foregoing is proven property. No such property, except proven acreage farm-outs, may be acquired without the specific consent of all of the Contributors and Davidson, Hartz, Hyde & Dewey, Inc. If so acquired, the cost and ownership thereof will be apportioned among Contributors and Blackwood & Nichols Company and Davidson, Hartz, Hyde & Dewey, Inc. as they shall agree.

It is emphasized that any venture in the oil business is a speculation and that funds contributed to it should be confined by a Contributor to an amount equal to income subject to high tax rates. A Contributor should not consider it an investment nor should he use investment capital, but his contribution should be limited to only a portion of his income for any one year.

THESE SECURITIES ARE OFFERED AS A SPECULATION

The date of this prospectus is November 28, 1950.

seven

....

A Winning Team

We have put together the best team in the oil patch.
F. G. "BLACKIE" BLACKWOOD

I n 1949, the estate planning needs of one of the Ball family's cousins set the stage for a change in direction in John's investment strategy. John Fisher visited with Paul Crosley about the need for his mother-in-law to begin planning her estate. Crosley recommended Clinton Davidson, who along with Raymond E. Hartz, had founded The Estate Planning Corporation & Fiduciary Counsel, a New York City firm established in 1925. Among its clients were many Eastern and Midwestern millionaires.

During Fisher's discussions with Davidson and Hartz, Fisher's business relationship with John came up and Fisher explained how he had been investing in the oil industry and producing a higher rate of after-tax return than most people enjoyed. Davidson and Hartz, always on the lookout for innovative ways to benefit their clients, asked for a meeting with John.

LEFT: The cover of the prospectus approved by the Securities and Exchange Commission in November, 1950, that allowed Blackwood & Nichols to fund the first federally-recognized joint venture in the history of oil and gas investment.

John and Blackie met Davidson at the Baker Hotel in Dallas. After listening to John explain the tax advantages, Davidson returned to New York City and discussed the concept with Hartz. Eventually, a joint venture was formed between Blackwood & Nichols and Davidson, Hartz, Hyde & Dewey, Inc.

Part of the Blackwood & Nichols winning team was W.J. "Bill" Hilseweck who graduated at the top of his class at the University of Oklahoma School of Geology. He was a vice president of Republic Natural Gas before he joined Blackwood & Nichols as a full partner in 1950.

The legal team that successfully prepared the huge number of legal documents to assist John in his ventures. Left to right, Kenneth McAfee, Richard "Dick" Taft, Joe Rucks, and Stuart Mark. McAfee began his law practice as a sole practitioner. When he and John met, McAfee shared a receptionist with Blackwood & Nichols.

Davidson realized that for the new company to succeed, two things were needed. First, sufficient capital was necessary to drill a great number of wells. Second, only experienced operators of unquestioned reliability must be employed to locate the oil and drill the wells.[1]

To convince one of his chief investors to invest money in the project, Davidson met with him to explain the advantages of investing in oil and natural gas exploration. Davidson realized that if he could convince one investor to participate, others would follow. After listening, the investor agreed, but only if, Davidson, Hartz, Hyde & Dewey, Inc., with their experience in financial management and tax planning, supervised the operation. Davidson, Hartz, Hyde & Dewey, in turn, planned to rely on Blackwood & Nichols.

With their newfound Wall Street partners, John and Blackie formalized their agreement and created an Oklahoma partnership called Blackwood & Nichols Company, on April 15, 1949. The original investors were John Fisher, John and Mary Nichols, and F. G. and Dola Blackwood. However, Bill and Helen McCauley Hilseweck joined the firm just as it was being formed. After serving as head of Gulf Oil's West Texas Geological Office for years, Hilseweck had moved to Dallas to become vice president of Republic Natural Gas Company. John persuaded Hilseweck to leave the gas company and become part of Blackwood & Nichols.[2] Hilseweck's geological expertise was so valued that he and his wife Helen were given a quarter interest in the new company.

It was an unstoppable team. Hilseweck was an expert geologist; Blackie was a veteran driller; and John had become a master salesman and accounting and tax expert.

Both the Davidson investment firm and Blackwood & Nichols agreed that the next step was to register their drilling funds with the Securities and Exchange Commission (SEC), in Washington, D.C. Such registration, they believed, was vital to establish credibility with wealthy investors. However, when John approached SEC officials, he was rebuffed. The investment proposal was not a security, the SEC officials maintained, and therefore there was no need to register. In addition, none of the SEC's standard forms applied to the limited partnership concept.

Fortunately, John persuaded the SEC officials to give him forms for stocks and bonds. Once he received the forms, John realized that he needed legal help and turned to Oklahoma

City attorney and CPA Kenneth McAfee, whose office was across the hall from the Blackwood & Nichols office in the Liberty Bank Building.

Working quickly, McAfee put a prospectus together, and then, working closely with Don Hyde, of Davidson, Hartz, Hyde & Dewey, pursued SEC registration through three amendments. McAfee proved so valuable that John retained him as the company attorney and for his personal legal work.

When the SEC regulators realized that registration of oil deals would be a form of protection for investors, in what had been to that point a business plagued by outrageous promises and even swindles, they became enthusiastic about John's concept. On November 28, 1950, SEC officials approved Registration No. 2-8663 that allowed the joint venture of Blackwood & Nichols Company and Davidson, Hartz, Hyde & Dewey, Inc., to sell $3.5 million "in oil property interests."[3]

The prospectus provided for a minimum investment of $5,000. Potential investors were warned, "These securities are offered as a speculation." There would be no underwriting discounts or commissions. However, Davidson's group would get one percent of the proceeds for offering expenses and Blackwood & Nichols would receive a monthly operating fee of $50 per well.[4]

On the first well of each prospect, the investors were to pay all acquisition costs on unproven acreage plus drilling and completion costs. Development costs on subsequent wells were to be divided 75 percent to the investors and 25 percent to the general partners, with revenues split 62.5 percent to 37.5 percent. This first S-1 prospectus noted,

"There may be little or no recovery of the amounts invested by Contributors."[5]

Two decades after the SEC approval, Truman E. Anderson, Jr., in his book, *Oil Program Investments,* wrote, "This first offering was obviously an oil program, but it certainly was unusual by current standards…The prospectus contained no information on possible conflicts of interest, and almost nothing was said about the risks of oil program investments. Nonetheless it was an important step in the history of oil investments, because it was the first program registered with the Securities and Exchange Commission and available by public offering in several states."[6]

Anderson said of the Blackwood & Nichols Company offering, "In structure, it was closer to a promoter's dream than a true oil program."[7]

John's investment idea had important advantages over the private deals of various independent operators. Still only a few people understood what an oil program was, a most obvious deterrent to sales growth. It took time for Blackwood & Nichols to make the idea acceptable, and the partners began to assemble a team to ensure its success.

Clinton Davidson advised John that because he was going to have a lot of influential people coming to see him, he should obtain more auspicious offices for Blackwood & Nichols. John and Blackie moved from their old quarters in the Liberty Bank Building to a more imposing office at the corner of Grand Boulevard and Robinson Avenue.

Next came the task of putting together a staff capable of implementing the new investment concept. John was the salesman who would raise the money. Blackie was in charge of engineering, with Bill Little and Dee Loos working under his supervision to oversee drilling. Bill Hilseweck located oil properties and did the geological work at drilling sites.

It was such a successful combination that between 1950 and 1953, Blackwood & Nichols exploded from 32 to more than 150 employees. Among the new workers was Cecelia "Peggy" Bowles, who for a time was both secretary and bookkeeper, until Bob Heston was hired as head of bookkeeping and accounting.[8]

Working with Heston were Bill Avery, Dick Bell, and Tommy Leflett. Joe Fred Gibson was the landman who, when everyone agreed on a property, went out and acquired mineral rights. John Roundtree was in charge of legal work.

Leflett also had the task of entering information on forms for each person who had a share of a well. In the precomputer age, it was a laborious undertaking. Each entry had to be figured by hand and typed on long tax forms. Because of the number of wells involved and the number of investors, bookkeeping was very time consuming. Money flowed in from each well and then had to be divided according to the amount invested by each participant. All bookkeeping work was done by hand in ledger books with only the aid of a ten-key adding machine. The bookkeeping had to be meticulous because everyone involved was trying to minimize taxes and was aware of IRS audits. Some of the books were kept in Durango, Colorado, and others in Midland, Texas, but all had to be coordinated from Oklahoma City.[9]

John's management style was simple. There were no big office meetings—no committees. John assigned people to jobs and let them do their work—he did not second-guess his employees. When someone proved unable to do his work, John got someone who could.

To hire the people he wanted, John offered top salaries. In addition, he allowed his employees, but not the partners, to invest their own money in mineral interests in areas near the wells the company was drilling.

John was extremely loyal to employees. Just six months after one employee went to work at Blackwood & Nichols, he was called back into service as a reserve officer during the Korean War. However, so that he would have a job when he returned, John did the man's work. John was proud of his people. He boasted, "We have been able to attract to our organization some of the best men in the oil industry."[10]

To fill secondary positions, John went to major universities and hired younger men of promise, offering them an opportunity with a growing company virtually free of red tape. The policy paid handsome dividends. For example, Dick Haag was hired as a newly-graduated geologist from the University of Oklahoma. His first job was to "sit" on a well in West Texas as it was being drilled. When he arrived on the site, it was still at a shallow depth. Haag sampled the mud periodically and checked the drilling bit's progress through the top layers of the formation. When the well was near its intended depth of 11,500 to 12,000 feet, a more experienced geologist was to be assigned.

One day, as Haag was sitting on the well and munching on a sandwich, he suddenly realized that "the earth is nothing more than a geologic sandwich. The pieces of bread are the layers of sand, gravel, and mud—while the meat is the oil. If I can bite through the sandwich and not taste the meat, why couldn't we be drilling through oil sand and miss it?"[11]

With that thought, Haag began taking samples more often. At 5,000 feet, he told the astonished crew, "We've hit oil!" He was right. He had found production from an unexpected zone.

Mary dressed John in the finest suits to make a good impression upon the wealthy potential investors he called upon.

eight

The Lure of Tax Breaks

I didn't have to talk about how good the oil or gas production might be, the tax advantage was the big selling point to investors.

JOHN W. NICHOLS

With the best available and most motivated employees in place, it was time to sell John's idea to potential investors. It was Davidson's job to introduce John to the wealthiest Americans.

For investors, John targeted individuals who had annual salaries of $400,000 to $500,000 or an equivalent income that put them in the top tax bracket. Davidson would contact such people and tell them, "Bring your accountant, your CPA, to meet with John Nichols. Listen to him. Ask him questions. Have your CPA ask him questions. Then make your own decision."[1] Because of his years of estate planning, Davidson was able to get big-name investors to listen. John Fisher, through his personal and family contacts, also lined John up with potential investors.

After Davidson opened doors, John traveled to various cities to "sell the deal." He succeeded most of the time because of thorough preparation. He knew the background of the people he was seeing and did his homework. He always presented *pro formas*, detailed budgets, and other information so he could provide projections for the investment prospects. In addition, he always had alternate propositions if the first or second did not interest the potential investor. Fisher recalled, "What set John apart was a combination of his ability to know the customers and to inform them very well of what he was doing. Plus he had a record to go by. And he totally believed in what he was doing. He had confidence."[2]

Some investors were reluctant because of the absence of any competition. When considering investments, they liked to compare one against another. As Benjamin F. Fairless, president of Bethlehem Steel, told John, "I don't like this program because you're the only card game in town. I can say yes or I can say no, but I can't say I like your program better than I do another." However, Fairless did invest, as did others.[3]

What really intrigued potential investors was John's plan of using profits and tax savings from conservative drilling to offset any wildcat exploration. The result was "riskless oil speculation," a term Blackwood & Nichols used in a brochure explaining the investment program.

The concept was simple. Approximately 40 percent of each drilling fund was used to drill wells in proven territory, where statistics showed that three of four wells drilled were likely to be productive. Because the average cost of drilling a well was about $100,000 at the time, a fund of $1 million, using 40 percent for conservative drilling, would allow four wells to be drilled, three of which would most likely be productive. Their value then would be $300,000 each, at a minimum, plus there would be tax credits of $241,800. Then the remaining $600,000 would be used for wildcat drilling. If all the holes were dry, there still was a large tax credit, bringing the total value produced by the million-dollar drilling fund to a minimum of $1,009,800, counting tax write-offs and the value of the producing wells.[4]

Fund 1, the first effort of the joint venture, was sold to a virtual "Who's Who" of American business and industry. Among them were the Badenhausens of Ballantine Brewery in Newark, New Jersey; the Uihleins of Milwaukee, Wisconsin's Schlitz Brewery; F. Alex Nason and others in Luberzahl Corporation of Cleveland, Ohio; Herbert F. Johnson of S.C. Johnson & Son Inc. in Racine, Wisconsin; Colonel Willard F. Rockwell, Sr., of what is now Rockwell International Corporation in Pittsburgh, Pennsylvania; the Pillsbury family of Minneapolis, Minnesota; and top executives at Chrysler Corporation and General Motors Corporation. In addition, there were numerous investors from the entertainment industry in Hollywood, California.

John made the Hollywood connection through James R. "Jim" McEldowney, a partner in the Oklahoma City insurance brokerage firm of Ansel, Earp, McEldowney and McWilliams. McEldowney had roomed at college with Robert Taylor who, in 1950, was one of the nation's top movie stars. Taylor asked McEldowney if he knew any way to help avoid heavy taxes and McEldowney told him about Blackwood & Nichols. Taylor invested in the venture and told other film personalities about the possibilities.

Many of the movie stars employed A. Morgan Maree, Jr., & Associates, a financial management company in Los Angeles, California. Soon the company summoned John to the West Coast to explain his plan. Among the Hollywood investors, in addition to Taylor, were Walter Pidgeon, June Allyson, Dick Powell, Ginger Rogers, and Barbara Stanwick. Taylor came to

Actor Robert Taylor, left, was the star of a party at the Nichols' home in Oklahoma City. Taylor was one of many Hollywood stars who took advantage of the tax breaks offered by John's investment strategy. At the party, Kent Nichols, age 5, did not recognize the clean-shaven Taylor because he had seen the actor recently in a movie in which Taylor wore a long beard.

Oklahoma City on occasion to look after his investments—and to go quail hunting with Blackie and John.

The minimum amount accepted from a single investor, according to the Fund 1 prospectus, was $5,000, but John decided the actual "self-imposed minimum" was $25,000. The largest single investor was W. I. F. Sun, a Chinese businessman. Sun's unique approach almost overwhelmed John. Sun arrived in John's Oklahoma City office, opened his briefcase, and counted out $300,000 in cash. Clinton Davidson speculated that the money actually was from Madame Chiang Kai-Shek, wife of the leader of the Nationalist Chinese.[5]

Fund 1 closed at $1,430,000, although the prospectus allowed up to $3.5 million. In line with the conservative approach promised, about 40 percent was invested in oil properties in Andrews, Upton, and Gaines counties in the Permian Basin of West Texas. It was a proven field where the success ratio was excellent. When the wells produced as expected, they brought a stream of low-tax revenue to the partners and the investors in Fund 1.

With the remainder of the money, the joint partners decided to drill in the Northeast Blanco Field in New Mexico, a decision with unexpected long-range consequences. The venture was a farm-out from Standard Oil of Indiana (Stanolind), in San Juan and Rio Arriba counties, New Mexico.

Northeast Blanco was nothing but a lot of open land in the rough country of extreme northwestern New Mexico. Some of the land belonged to the federal government, some to the state, and some to private citizens. Only a portion of the area was under lease to Stanolind which proposed to give half its lease acreage to Republic Natural Gas if Republic purchased the remaining acreage in the basin to form a "unit."[6]

Stanolind's geologists already had reported there was a high probability of natural gas being found in the area. However, both the demand for natural gas and its price, 12 to 13 cents per thousand cubic feet (MCF), were depressed. Likewise, the field seemed so remote that getting gas to market would cost more than the production would be worth. To some of Stanolind geologists, the Northeast Blanco Field was "the largest 'non-commercial' gas field in the world."[7]

The Northeast Blanco opportunity came to Blackwood & Nichols because of Bill Hilseweck, who was still at Republic Natural Gas when he completed his geological fieldwork on the field in 1949. Hilseweck reported that he believed the area was a good prospect that could result in a financial bonanza. However, his recommendation was ignored. Hilseweck then asked if he could tell John and Blackie about his findings. He was told, "If you want to do your friend the worst favor in the world, tell him to buy it."[8]

Undaunted, Hilseweck telephoned John, who already had asked him to become a partner in Blackwood & Nichols. He accepted John's offer and said, "Here's the first deal. You ought to take it [the Northeast Blanco] and drill it."[9]

Based on Hilseweck's recommendation, the old unincorporated partnership of Blackwood, Nichols, and Fisher accepted a farm-out from Stanolind. Half the acreage under lease by Stanolind came to them free. Money from the first drilling fund was used by May of 1952 to purchase the remaining acreage in what became known as the Northeast Blanco Unit. Blackwood, Nichols, and Fisher eventually purchased an interest in a total of 32 sections of land.

While John pondered the future of the Northeast Blanco Unit, Fund 1 had been subscribed, and with monies from it, a contract was drawn to sink the first well to the Dakota formation in the San Juan Basin in New Mexico. Overseeing the fieldwork for Blackwood & Nichols was Delasso "Dee" Loos, who had been in charge of wells in the vicinity of Midland for Blackwood & Nichols since 1950. However, in May, 1952, he moved his family to Durango, Colorado, the nearest city of any size to the Northeast Blanco Unit. During this time, Loos was under the immediate supervision of Bill Little. Under Loos' direction, the hole was pushed into the Dakota formation and then shot with nitroglycerin. It proved to be a fair producer of natural gas.

As the drill stem went down in the first Northeast Blanco well, it passed through a large 40-foot thick seam of coal, known as Fruitland Coal, at a depth of 3,500 feet. As the drill bit passed through the coal seam, the crew increased the weight of the mud to continue the drilling. Although the water "would gurgle, and every once in a while come out the top of the well," Loos managed to hold the gas down until the drill bit hit the top of the Mackenburg formation.[10]

When they first hit the coal seam, Hilseweck told anyone who would listen that someday the coal would be the source of a lot of gas. At the time, however, the gas in the coal was not considered profitable because of the large amount of water coming to the surface with it. The method to remove gas from coal was still two decades from being discovered.[11]

Once four wells had been drilled in the

Blackwood & Nichols employee Dee Loos was so revered in the Navajo Lake region of northwest New Mexico that the main road into the area was named for him. Loos loved the area so much that he continued to live there after he retired. *Courtesy Devon Energy Corporation.*

5,000-feet zone and gas reserves proven, John opened talks with El Paso Natural Gas Company (El Paso), the major gas purchaser in the area. With lawyer Kenneth McAfee doing the negotiating, a tentative agreement was worked out with El Paso. A new company, Northeast Blanco Development Corporation, was established to borrow $19 million at 4.5 percent interest from El Paso and lay a pipeline to the field. To service both debt and interest, El Paso received 9.5 cents on each MCF the company purchased. The Northeast Blanco Development Corporation received 3.5 cents.

At the time, El Paso Natural Gas was trying to get permission from the Federal Power Commission to lay a pipeline through the San Juan Basin. However, the company had to show it had sufficient dedicated natural gas to service the lines.

To satisfy the requirement, El Paso was purchasing natural gas wells from area producers once the wells were drilled. This left the producers with an override royalty interest that sometimes was nearly as large as a full working interest. Such an arrangement was known as a Gas Lease Agreement (GLA). Blackwood & Nichols entered into several GLAs with El Paso.

Because the price of natural gas was so low, the cash flow from the Northeast Blanco at first was skimpy. However, it was producing from what was known to be an extremely large field and the pipeline into the area meant there was a buyer for any additional output found. Using money from Fund 1 and money borrowed from El Paso, additional wells were drilled in the years that followed. By 1965, almost 65 wells had been completed with not a single dry hole.[12]

Low wellhead prices meant there was no incentive to continue drilling in the Northeast Blanco except for what was necessary to retain the leases. Even with low prices, a small profit was being shown and the $19 million loan from El Paso Natural Gas was paid off in 1973.

The original investors in Fund 1 also had income from properties in the West Texas Sprayberry Field. The money returned by wells in the Sprayberry Field and those in the Northeast Blanco, along with depreciation allowances, tax deductions, and capital gains, meant the investors were receiving a healthy return—and would continue to do so in the years ahead.

The investors in Fund 1 were so pleased with their return that selling of subsequent funds proved to be easier. By 1958, eight funds had been sold, an average of about one a year. Each was for approximately $1 million. The total amount available for drilling in each fund was used before another fund was offered. In fact, to attain maximum tax benefits, all the money in a fund had to be expended within one year. Also, all the investors in a fund were prohibited from beginning a separate project until a fund had been organized and all the money spent.[13]

In each of the eight funds, the identical, careful approach was used. Forty percent of the money was used to drill in known producing areas, and the remainder was spent on more speculative ventures. By the time the tenth well was drilled in the Northeast Blanco, at a cost of $3.5 million, the field had produced natural gas worth $17 million. Of course, a lion's share of the income went to El Paso Natural Gas, but the investors received excellent dividends in addition to their tax write-offs.

In 2004, more than 50 years after drilling began in the Northeast Blanco Unit, early investors continued to recapture the amount of their original investment every four months—making the Fund 1 investment the most successful and lucrative oil and gas venture in history. Ten new wells were drilled in the unit in 2003.

nine

Diversified
Investments

*I have enough of this world's goods.
It's time to give it to my kids.*

F. G. "BLACKIE" BLACKWOOD

I n 1957, *Blackie Blackwood decided to retire* and distribute
his wealth to his children. To do so, he wanted to divest
his holdings in Blackwood & Nichols, with the exception
of the Northeast Blanco Unit, and place them into trusts for his
children. The only way this could be done was to dissolve the
partnership.

The other three partners, Fisher, Hilseweck, and John,
agreed, and the split was made. The three remaining partners put their Blackwood & Nichols' holdings, except for
the Northeast Blanco, in a new partnership they called
FHN, Ltd. Then the four original partners put their assets
from Fund 1, which owned a 25 percent working interest
in Northeast Blanco, into a newly organized Blackwood &
Nichols Company, Limited, which was operated by Charles
F. Blackwood, Blackie's son. The new company maintained

offices in the First National Bank Building in downtown Oklahoma City.

In anticipation of Blackie's retirement, John formed Nichols Exploration Company. The following year, 1958, he organized a new company, Mid-America Minerals, Inc., along with John Fisher, William M. "Bill" Avery, Bill Little, F. Alex Nason, H. Campbell Stuckeman, Lou Wilson, and others. John was named president.

Next door to Mid-America Minerals' office in the old Liberty National Bank Building was the Oklahoma City office of the Tulsa-based Calvert Exploration Company, owned by Tony and Allen Calvert. In 1965, Mid-America Minerals was merged into the Calvert Exploration Company. Eventually the larger Calvert Exploration Company was sold to Sun Oil Company at a handsome return for the original investors in Mid-America Minerals.[1]

John also was involved in numerous other projects. He continued to manage the Lillian W. Simpson Trust and he oversaw investments in various pieces of real estate and other financial ventures. In fact, one of these separate investments proved spectacularly successful.

Through a friend, Art Wood, Nichols learned about Pacific Properties, a company in Hawaii that had land for sale. Pacific Properties also owned a television station, a CBS affiliate, but, as with most television ventures in that era, the station was losing money. However, it was drive-in theaters that Pacific Properties owned on fee land all over Hawaii that caught John's attention. There was little privately-owned land in Hawaii and John recognized the opportunity to acquire valuable fee simple property and moved quickly.

First, he and Wood negotiated an option to purchase Pacific Properties. In Oklahoma City, Nichols found three investors willing to take the risk with him. They put up $150,000 to secure an option on Pacific Properties. John then borrowed $8 million to complete the purchase. Within 18 months, the television station and properties had been sold and each partner realized a return of $1.8 million dollars on their investments.[2]

As a CPA John was aware that many physicians in Oklahoma City were looking for ways to shelter part of their income. Even before the flow of federal dollars into the health field began in the mid-1960s, doctors had relatively high incomes but usually no expertise in accounting and investments. That made them prime prospects for John's investment programs.

"In my life," John explained, "I've become involved in situations where, all of a sudden, a door would open. Sometimes before I could get through that door, another door would open, showing me the way the Lord wanted me to go."[3]

A particular opportunity began on December 2, 1949, when a group of physicians in Oklahoma City organized the Pasteur Medical Building Corporation (PMBC). Capitalized at $300,000, its purpose was to acquire and manage real estate.

Dr. Gerald Rogers was elected president, Dr. Don H. O'Donoghue was chosen vice president, and Alfred H. Smith was named secretary and treasurer. Joining them on PMBC's Board of Directors were Dr. George S. Bozalis and Dr. Ray M. Balyeat. Smith was the administrator of the Oklahoma City Allergy Clinic in which Dr. Bozalis was a partner. The other three were physicians practicing in Oklahoma City. Other stockholders included Dr. John Bozalis, Dr. Vernon Cushing, Dr. George Kimball, Dr. William L. Bond, Dr. D. Patrick O'Donoghue, Dr. William T. Snoddy, Dr. Herbert Kent, Dr. Kenneth Bohan, Dr. Moorman P. Prosser, Dr. Coye W. McClure, Dr. Rex E. Kenyon, and Dr. Robert Ellis.

The initial $100,000 of stock sales was used to purchase the Pasteur Medical Building at Northwest 10th Street and Lee in Oklahoma City. Just across the street from St. Anthony Hospital, and near three other hospitals, it was the largest medical care facility in Oklahoma County at that time. Because of its location, there was a waiting list for tenants.

Soon after PMBC purchased the Pasteur Building, a complete renovation was undertaken. When completed on November 1, 1951, the building was fully air conditioned, offered off-street parking, outdoor lighting, and self-service elevators. Seven years later, a new wing with five floors of office space, along with a parking deck, was added. A second above ground, covered parking deck was completed in the fall of 1965. The renovation and location of the Pasteur Building made it a lucrative investment.

Most members of PMBC shared membership in the Oklahoma City Golf and Country Club with John. Several of them had invested in his projects. Also, John owned sufficient stock in PMBC to serve on its board of directors. John already oversaw the corporation's books and leasing operations, and thus when the value of PMBC reached $3.3 million in the early 1960s, he proposed to use it as "equity money" to borrow against for drilling programs.

Previously, in the 1950s, John, his cousin Bill Whiteman, and a small group of Oklahoma City citizens had founded the Bank of MidAmerica Savings and Trust Company. John quickly discovered that almost all of Oklahoma's 500-plus banks were so small they could not afford the machinery to process their own checks or to perform many banking functions. Instead, they became affiliated with one of the four or five major state financial institutions and contracted for check processing and other services with the larger bank.

Each of the top Oklahoma banks was associated either with a family that had owned it for years or with a major company. In Oklahoma City, for example, Liberty National Bank, was closely associated with John's close friend, John Kirkpatrick, a major independent oilman; C. R. Anthony and his dry-goods store empire; Raymond A. Young and T.G.&Y., his national chain of variety stores; B. D. "Babe" Eddie and his Superior Feeds; and other major stockholders.

Liberty National Bank had been organized in Oklahoma City on September 3, 1918, by a group of local businessmen who capitalized it at $300,000 along with a surplus of $30,000. They elected L. T. Simmons its first president, and the day it opened, $726,265 was deposited. Simmons proved conservative with investors' and depositors' money during the boom following World War I, but still doubled Liberty's assets by 1921. That same conservative management was followed during the giddy years of the Roaring Twenties, and thus during the Great Depression, Liberty continued to pay dividends and protect depositors' accounts. Liberty not only survived the depression, but also absorbed several other Oklahoma City financial institutions, such as the Oklahoma State Bank, the Oklahoma National Bank, and the Oklahoma Stockyards National Bank.

Liberty also acquired the bank with which John was associated, the Bank of MidAmerica, by issuing additional shares of Liberty stock to the owners of the Bank of MidAmerica. Thus, John became a shareholder in Liberty. In so doing he became well acquainted with its president, Harvey Everest, and its executive vice president, Morrison Tucker.

In 1962, John was walking down the street when he met Tucker. The two men stopped to visit and Tucker seemed upset. John asked, "What's the matter, Tuck?" Tucker replied, "Well, the control of Liberty National Bank is about to disappear to a group in Minnesota." Tucker then explained that approximately 20 percent of the bank shares, most of which belonged to

C. R. Anthony, was being offered for sale and if the shares were sold, most other major investors would also sell.[4]

Finally Tucker asked John, "Why don't you buy it—or see if you can get some of your friends to buy it?" Believing his friend was jesting, John replied, "Good grief, I can't buy it." However, John was intrigued and learned from Tucker that it would require about $4.5 million to acquire the stock.[5]

After completing his conversation with Tucker, John went to see John Kirkpatrick, who listened and then said, "Let's go and see if we can't get it." Together they met with Anthony, B.D. Eddie, Harvey Everest, and others who agreed to sell their stock for about $4 million. Kirkpatrick then asked John, "How are we going to pay for it?"[6]

John consulted with H. Campbell "Cal" Stuckeman, Sam R. Raymond, John W. Fisher, Edmund F. Ball, and other close friends who agreed to invest in Liberty's purchase. John also called on Nick Bailey, an investment banker at New York City's Chemical Bank, who suggested using PMBC stock as leverage for the purchase.

Following Bailey's suggestion, John pledged PMBC's stock to an insurance company in Nashville, Tennessee, for the money to purchase the Liberty stock. In addition, he refinanced a $3.3 million loan on the Pasteur Medical Building Complex with Massachusetts Mutual Life Insurance Company and issued additional stock in PMBC. Doctor-tenants in the Pasteur Building, who had been unable to buy an interest in the original corporation, purchased some of the new PMBC stock. Additional shares were sold to other physicians in Oklahoma City.

Using the $6 million he had raised, John and Kirkpatrick bought 100,000 shares, valued at $60 per share of Liberty stock by December 28, 1962. The purchase gave them control of approximately 17 percent of the bank's outstanding stock and necessitated the changing of PMBC's corporate purpose to include investing in stocks, bonds, and other securities.

John was elected a director in the newly reorganized PMBC. He then entered into a joint venture agreement with John Kirkpatrick, Morrison Tucker, Sam Raymond, Cal Stuckeman, John Fisher, and Edmund Ball to bring together such a significant block of Liberty National stock to gain effective control of the bank. Also, nearly all of PMBC's stockholders transferred their accounts to Liberty.

Liberty's stock tripled in value and by 1963, the bank grew from the fourth to the second largest in Oklahoma with deposits of $266,712,928. The value of PMBC's investment in Liberty also had grown. The corporation's 100,000 shares of stock, purchased on December 28, 1962, had increased to 127,118 shares by January 15, 1963. With a 27 percent stock dividend, the adjusted value of $47 a share already had increased to $54 by July 19, 1963, and was paying ten cents a share dividend each month. At $54 a share, PMBC had realized a paper profit of $800,000 in less than seven months, in addition to a 25 cents per share annual earning derived from the buildings the bank owned.

In January, 1963, an offer was made to PMBC's Board of Directors to purchase 24,000 PMBC shares of Liberty National Bank stock at $100 a share. Charles Dewey opposed the sale, arguing that in all probability the stock would double in five years. Other members of the board agreed and the offer was declined. By 1965, the PMBC share of Liberty stock had a market value of $7,744,744, while PMBC stock had increased 50 percent in value. In the years that followed, Liberty continued to be highly profitable as it added new programs, such as the Liberty Card, one of Oklahoma's first credit cards.

The North African country of Libya was home to Sahara Oilfield Services (S.O.S.) operations.

t e n

....

S.O.S.

If any investor was uncomfortable with the risks,
I wanted him to be able to get out of the venture—
and still make a profit.

JOHN W. NICHOLS

By the late 1950s, John's investments and businesses were varied—but all in America. That is, until the formation of Sahara Oilfield Services Company (SOS).

The investment in SOS grew out of John's membership in Risk Capital, an investment organization in Oklahoma City that met once a month. Risk Capital had two members each from a variety of business or professions—automobile sales, insurance, real estate, oil and gas production, banking, and accounting—who would meet and discuss their investments. John and Bill Majors were the two members from the oil and gas industry.

Early in 1959, Majors was visited by Fred Mace who had been working for Continental Oil Company (Conoco) in Houston, Texas. Conoco was pulling out of the Middle East for political reasons. However, Mace was convinced there would be continued oil drilling in the region, especially in Libya, and he wanted to form a company to sell oil field supplies and services to the oil firms that he believed would do business there.

Libya was ruled by King Sayyid Muhammed al-Idris who had ascended to the throne seven years earlier. His kingdom was among the world's poorest countries, with 1.5 million people and just $9 million in exports, mostly olive oil, peanuts, tomatoes, and scrap metal salvaged from the debris of World War II battles. Libya had an average income of less than $50 per person.

However, during the 1950s, major international oil firms, particularly American companies, had begun exploring along the north shore of Africa in the hope of matching major discoveries in Saudi Arabia and Kuwait. Anticipating the best, King Idris issued Royal Decree Number 25 stating that all subsurface deposits belonged to the state, and the government would get 50 percent of all income after operating costs were deducted.[1]

Also the king's edict said any company doing business in Libya had to have 51 percent Libyan ownership. In addition, there was an unwritten law that once a Libyan was hired, he could be fired only under rare circumstances. Despite these rigid conditions, Libya actually gave great latitude to oil companies that quickly moved into the country. Among the companies were Standard of New Jersey, later Esso, then Exxon; Royal Dutch Shell; British Petroleum; Gulf Oil; Texaco; Standard Oil of California or Chevron; and Mobil.

Mace believed that the major oil firms would not want to import their own supplies to Libya because it would force them to hire a large number of Libyans who could not be fired. Instead, he believed the companies would buy from a service company, especially one operated by longtime members of the oil fraternity. Mace hoped to first gain the Hughes Tool Company's Libyan account and then, he thought, other manufacturers would sign up.[2]

Majors listened and then asked Mace how much start up money was needed. Armed with this information, Majors invited John and several other friends to a luncheon meeting at Oklahoma City's Skirvin Hotel. All in attendance agreed to participate and the new organization was named Sahara Oilfield Services Company of Libya, Ltd.

Mace was sent to Libya to begin SOS's local operations. To satisfy the 51 percent Libyan ownership requirement, Mace chose the five Serrag brothers, all highly successful Libyan businessmen. Because of tax benefits, Majors and his partners formed Tau, Incorporated, a Panamian corporation, to handle the remaining 49 percent.

Mace's timing was excellent. On April 18, 1959, an Esso well, the Zelten Number 1, began producing 17,000 barrels of oil per day from a depth of just 6,000 feet.

Shortly thereafter, Zelten Number 2 was completed at 15,000 barrels a day. These and other discoveries confirmed Libya's tremendous oil potential, and by 1962, the country was producing a million barrels of oil per day. At the same time, most of the major firms were purchasing supplies and services from SOS. Unfortunately, SOS remained "pretty shaky" financially.[3]

From 1959 to 1963, John had been a stockholder in SOS but had little to do with its day-to-day management. He was aware that the company was suffering from poor management and thought it could be made profitable by following correct business procedures. When Major suggested selling SOS, John immediately thought about the possibility of PMBC as a buyer. He persuaded PMBC's Board of Directors to pay $600,000 to acquire Tau, Incorporated.

John intended to put SOS on sound business practices that would allow it to begin producing dividends to reduce the $600,000 investment in Tau. Once $600,000 in profits had been generated, hopefully within three years, John believed that SOS could be sold for at least $1 million.

As John studied Sahara's operations, he decided that a major part of the problem was Fred Mace and that SOS needed an on-the-scene comptroller. John and Majors selected Sy Helm who at the time was working for Eddie Chiles' Western Oil Company in Fort Worth, Texas. Helm agreed, and when Mace was killed in a car accident shortly thereafter, Helm replaced him as Sahara's chief of operations in Libya.

John's plan for SOS concentrated on three areas. First, SOS was a manufacturer's representative for such companies as Black, Sivalls & Bryson; Hughes Tool Company; Lufkin Foundry & Machine Company; Milwhite Mud Sales; Oil Center Tool Company; Chicksan-Weco; Byron Jackson; Brown-Boveri; and Waukesha Motor Company that supplied necessary oil field supplies and technology. In addition, it represented General Electric, which supplied mobile communications equipment. SOS also owned and operated Power Casing Tong Service.

Second, SOS was a material handling and warehousing contractor for almost every major oil company in Libya. Its clients included Mobil; American Overseas Petroleum, owned jointly by Standard Oil of California and Texaco; Oasis Oil Company of Libya, the operating company for Amerada/Hess, Conoco, and Marathon; and the Libyan Pan American Oil Company.

Third, SOS continued its contract to maintain all base communications equipment for American forces at Wheelus Air Force Base, east of Tripoli, and to install the automation system at the Oasis Oil Company's field at Dahra.

Sahara Oilfield Services operated in the northern African country of Libya in the 1950s and 1960s. It was not unusual for John to encounter a herd of camels en route to SOS warehouses scattered throughout the country.

SOS also helped oil companies in Libya obtain necessary licenses and permits, maintained several highly mobile hydraulic power-actuated, casing-tong units, and had skilled operators to assist oil companies with installation of casing in wells. To accomplish all these tasks, SOS operated warehouses in Tripoli, Benghazi, and Agedabia, along with its offices in Tripoli and Benghazi. All the warehouses and offices were linked by radio to each other and to the various oil fields, enabling its personnel to communicate from their offices to all drilling, production, and pipeline stations in the desert. At its Tripoli and Benghazi offices, SOS also maintained accounting sections to handle material inventories and billings as well as money transfers.

John also sought to expand Sahara's business in Libya through his acquaintances in the international oil fraternity.

One contact was E. J. Jameson, manager of the Material and Purchasing Department of Esso Europe, a subsidiary of Exxon. Through Jameson, John inquired about having Sahara supply tubular goods to Esso's Libyan operations. The two men arrived at "a shake hands deal" to that effect, and in January, 1964, John flew to London to sign the contract with Esso.

Mary accompanied John to London. And, because there would be endless typing and paperwork, he also took his secretary, Ruth Kay.[4]

Thinking he would be in London for only a week or two, John checked into a local hotel. However, he quickly discovered that Esso executives were not as interested in doing business as he was. Although they were in no position to say no, they did not have to say yes immediately and the negotiations began to drag out.

The SOS warehouse in Libya provided supplies and equipment needed by American oil companies to tap the large reserves of oil beneath the Libyan sand.

When Mary learned that the negotiations were going to take months to complete, she suggested finding an apartment or flat. John agreed and they soon found a two-bedroom flat at 49 Hill Street. Shortly afterward, John also rented an office for Sahara in Hanover Square, opposite the Esso Europe offices.

Arrangements at the flat had John and Mary sleeping in one bedroom and Ruth sleeping in the other. Mary and Ruth became close friends. However, one of the doormen for the building in which the flat was located noticed that at times John left the building with Ruth and at other times with Mary. There was a good reason—Mary prepared breakfast and then John and Ruth left for work.

Occasionally, when going to dinner or to some evening event, John would have both women with him. Not knowing the actual situation, the doorman was impressed with John, finally asking him how he was able to keep two women happy.[5]

It took six months of negotiations before John was able to conclude an agreement providing for Sahara to supply all tubular goods for Esso's drilling in Libya. Thanks to that deal and to improved management and cost control, SOS declared a dividend of $110,000 in 1964. There was another dividend of $90,000 in 1965 and a third in 1966 of $58,000.

In addition to purchasing and operating Sahara Oilfield Services, John also acquired several other oil-related firms for PMBC. One company was Lucey Products Corporation, which had been started in 1908 when Captain John Francis Lucey founded J. F. Lucey, Inc., to sell and service rotary drilling equipment. The firm eventually moved to Pittsburgh and produced a rotary rig well known throughout the industry. In 1933, the company stopped manufacturing rigs and began representing various manufacturers of rotary rigs worldwide.

In 1965, John learned that Franklin E. Bernsen was ready to sell his controlling interest in Lucey Products, and with approval of the board of directors, PMBC paid $1,232,750 for the company in July, 1965. The purchase price was approximately $100,000 less than the book value of its assets. Immediately the old Delaware corporation was dissolved and its assets were transferred to a wholly owned subsidiary of PMBC named Lucey Products Corporation, chartered in Oklahoma. John also acquired Pathfinder, which had been formed in 1965 by George P. Daley to sell oilfield supplies in Nigeria.

Some of PMBC's shareholders were unsure about its expansion into the foreign oil business even though PMBC continued to show good profits under John's leadership. They believed that PMBC had become too diversified and that the company's board of directors had expanded too rapidly and included too many bankers and oil men. The oil business, particularly in foreign countries, presented tremendous risks, an uncomfortable feeling to many of the shareholders.

By the fall of 1965, John was aware of the growing restlessness among PMBC shareholders. He always believed that any investor who was unhappy should be allowed to leave the enterprise and also realize a profit. So he decided the time had come to allow those who wanted to get out of banking and the oil business to do so.

As its CEO, John sent a letter to all PMBC shareholders in November, 1965. The letter carefully outlined the risks of overseas oil investment, including governmental instability. He offered several options for PMBC stockholders. They could take stock in PMBC as a subsidiary of Essex Corporation, a new

John and his investment group expanded into Nigeria in 1965. This photograph was taken on a trip to the capital city of Lagos. Left to right, John Kirkpatrick of Oklahoma City; John Nichols; the pilot; and Cal Stuckemen of Pittsburgh, Pennsylvania, whose wife was an heir to the Rockwell International fortune.

firm that would be created; they could take stock in the Liberty Corporation, likewise to be a subsidiary of Essex; or they could take stock in Essex itself.

On November 29, 1965, a specially called meeting of the PMBC shareholders was held. The name of the company was changed to Essex Corporation. The stockholders who did not want to be in banking and the oil business were given stock in PMBC in proportion to their share of assets in the previous company. Those who wanted to continue in the new direction took Essex stock, which owned the 138,000 shares of Liberty National Bank stock and Sahara Oilfield Services.

eleven
....

Essex

*By the 1960s, we had become diversified
and multinational in our business.*

JOHN W. NICHOLS

B y early 1965, the oil business in Libya was booming.
Some 20 American petroleum companies, along
with numerous foreign firms, had invested more
than $200 million in the North African desert kingdom in
search of hydrocarbons and were preparing to invest another
$200 million. More than 50 rigs were actively drilling and
overnight Libya had become a major source of petroleum
for Western Europe. The country had become the world's
fifth-largest oil exporting nation with exports of 627 million
barrels in 1965. It seemed there would be huge profits for
everyone.

   The Libyan government of King Sayyid Muhammed al-
Idris was receiving a 50 percent royalty on all oil income.
This represented more than 95 percent of Libya's total
exports and enabled King Idris' government to improve the
country's standard of living. However, Libya's government

believed it needed to increase its revenues and the only segment of the economy that could pay more was petroleum. In the summer of 1965, the government increased its share of royalties. The result was that by October, with profits squeezed, foreign oil companies in Libya reduced the number of active rigs to 20. The decrease in rig activity directly affected Sahara's profits.

During the time that Essex Corporation was performing oil field services for major companies in Libya through its subsidiary, Sahara, it also was trying to operate a similar business in the Federation of Nigeria. An offshore strike had been made in that African country's territorial waters in October, 1963, by American Overseas Petroleum, and by 1965, additional major discoveries had been made. In fact, every operator holding offshore acreage had struck oil with its first wells. By August 16, 1965, 16 fields had been found with a phenomenal success rate of 85 percent. As a result, Nigerian production jumped from 94,000 barrels per day in 1964 to 285,000 barrels per day in 1965.

On October 18, 1965, George Daley told John that he believed there was an opportunity for Essex to form a subsidiary to do in Nigeria what Sahara was doing in Libya. Because of its remoteness, Nigeria had been by-passed by most service companies for more accessible and active areas such as the North Sea, Libya, and the Persian Gulf. With the exception of Shell-British Petroleum, no oil company had a complete engineering staff in Nigeria.[1]

John quickly proposed the Nigerian venture to the Essex Board of Directors which, on December 29, 1965, voted to form Trans-Africa Engineering Services, a Nigerian corporation with offices in Lagos, to offer engineering and oil field services to the Nigerian petroleum industry. The new company had a board of six directors, three of whom by Nigerian law had to be citizens of that nation. The three American directors were John, John Kirkpatrick, and Ted Fendeiss.

The engineering firm of Butler, Miller & Lents of Houston, Texas, was retained to provide technical assistance to the Trans-Africa personnel. Harvey Atkinson was named general manager for Trans-Africa, while Daley became supervisor of oil field services and the supply business for both Trans-Africa and other overseas Essex subsidiaries. Trans-Africa's personnel—geologists and petroleum, chemical, and natural gas engineers—served as oil and gas consultants, and performed feasibility and design studies for gathering, processing, and treating facilities for oil companies doing business in Nigeria. In addition, Trans-Africa acted as service representatives for the same suppliers and manufacturers as Sahara represented in Libya.

Trans-Africa officials quickly discovered it was difficult to do business in Nigeria. Although it was one of the most populous countries in Africa, and was endowed with tremendous economic promise, it suffered from centuries-old tribal hatreds and rivalries. Just four days after Daley arrived in Nigeria, in January, 1966, an internal revolution enveloped the country, prompting John to remark, "I told George to stir up things in Nigeria, but I didn't mean start a revolution."[2]

Although Daley thought the political situation in Nigeria was "tenuous," he reported that he believed that oil development would continue because all the tribes involved in the civil war realized benefits from oil production. He also reported that there was "no anti-white feeling among the natives," and that special precautions, including armed guards, were taken to protect foreigners.[3]

Despite several coups in Nigeria, major oil companies continued to operate their drilling rigs—and Trans-Africa was servicing 31 of them. However, by May 24, 1967, Daley was convinced that the civil unrest in Nigeria had basically shut down Trans-Africa's business.[4] Fortunately, the situation in Nigeria began to improve in 1968, and there was a resulting upturn in oil exploration. By July 24, 1968, Trans-Africa was breaking even.

In the spring of 1966, Essex Corporation also was attempting to open sales to Esso Europe, which controlled more than 50 corporations, many of which were involved in drilling in the North Sea. Sahara Oilfield Services previously had furnished some tubular goods to Esso. However, because Sahara was 51 percent owned by the Serrag brothers of Libya, more than half of the profit from sales to Esso was not going to Essex.

George Daley and Ted Fendeiss met with E. J. Jameson of Esso Europe to explore the possibility of opening direct sales to Esso and other European operators. On September 21, 1966, Daley informed the Essex board that an investment of $300 million in equipment and supplies during the next year could result in a potential profit of 15 to 20 percent and recommended the expenditure of $50,000 to open a London office under the supervision of Fendeiss. On May 24, 1967, Essply Limited, a United Kingdom corporation, was formed to furnish tubular goods and other supplies to Esso and other companies operating in Europe and Africa.

As part of the effort to increase sales in the North Sea area, John acquired 40 percent of Offshore Drilling Supplies,

Ltd. (ODS), a British concern owned by Michael Huntley-Robertson, located at Great Yarmouth, on September 2, 1967, at a cost of $56,000. Offshore Drilling Supplies gave Essex an entry into the North Sea area at a nominal cost, with the added benefit that funds were used to double the working capital of an existing company.

Huntley-Robertson's company not only provided a mechanism to increase sales of oil field supplies, his incredible knowledge of people in the oil industry helped John in several ways. He was born in Argentina where his father was a British Secret Service agent. After spending years in school in England, Huntley-Robertson took a job at age 16 as an apprentice oil driller in Peru. For a decade he worked for oil service companies such as Halliburton.[5]

After working for Gardner-Denver, a major supplier of oil field equipment, for several years in Canada, Alaska, and South America, Huntley-Robertson founded ODS to service growing oil exploration efforts in the North Sea.[6]

Ted Fendeiss actually found Huntley-Robertson and introduced him to John for the first time at the Royal Garden Hotel in London on October 25, 1966. It was the beginning of a lifelong friendship between Huntley-Robertson and John, although Huntley-Robertson was at first a little unsure of the optimistic picture that John painted of oil and gas exploration potential in the United States.[7]

Another country into which Essex expanded its operations was Mexico. In 1967, John learned that Lucey Products was making limited sales to Pemex, the government owned corporation which totally controlled the petroleum industry in Mexico. After a careful investigation, he recommended that a Lucey Products subsidiary be established in Mexico. On September

18, 1967, Ess-Mex, S.A., a Mexican corporation, was formed with an initial investment of $16,000. Unfortunately, projected profits for Ess-Mex never materialized.

Essex Corporation—with John Nichols as CEO and chairman of the board—had become diversified and multinational. However, all the companies had a symbiotic relationship—each helping the other. Pathfinder manufactured oil field equipment and Lucey Products represented other manufacturers and suppliers of equipment used in oil fields. Sahara Oilfield Services, Trans-Africa Engineering, Offshore Drilling Supplies, and Ess-Mex sold the equipment either made by or distributed by one of the related companies.

All the operations required John's attention and time. It seemed as if he was in constant motion, traveling to England, Libya, Nigeria, or Mexico. Secretary Dorothy McDonald was in charge of making certain that John left Oklahoma City with a supply of the currency of the country he was visiting and a detailed portfolio of his business on that particular trip. McDonald maintained a "stash" of foreign currency to save John time in airports or banks in foreign countries.[8]

Between the trips, he attended board meetings in Oklahoma City and developed other areas of expansion for Essex Corporation.

One expansion for Essex was the 1966 purchase of KBMT-TV in Beaumont, on the Texas Gulf Coast. John already had nearly a decade of experience in the broadcast industry. He was an early investor in KOCO-TV in Enid, Oklahoma, an ABC affiliate that was the beneficiary of a special license issued by the Federal Communications Commission (FCC) for VHF channels in cities outside major metropolitan areas.

In 1958, KOCO-TV moved its tower to northwest

Oklahoma City. Its signal reached the more lucrative Oklahoma City market but could still be received by viewers in Enid, thereby complying with its FCC license. A new studio was built at Northwest 63rd Street and Portland Avenue and under the management of Ben K. West, KOCO-TV quickly became an industry mainstay.

In 1965, West was approached by the owners of KBMT-TV who had the same problem as KOCO-TV in Enid—a license in a smaller area that kept the station from being profitable. West reported the offer to John, but pointed out two problems with the purchase of KBMT-TV. First, he believed the station was plagued by management conflicts—second, its current tower was on the Gulf Coast, giving it a weak signal in Beaumont, making it difficult to compete with the NBC and CBS affiliates. However, with permission to move its tower already granted, West believed the second problem could be corrected. John concurred and also pointed out that KBMT-TV had another attractive feature—a substantial tax loss carry forward of nearly $700,000.

On January 19, 1966, KBMT's owners accepted Essex's offer of $562,500 for 45 percent of the outstanding stock of Television Broadcasters, the corporate owner of KBMT-TV. Essex's board approved the sale and committed $1,250,00 to purchase all outstanding KBMT-TV stock. However, that move was delayed until the station's tower was relocated.[9]

The purchase of the Texas television station was not extremely profitable for Essex. Unfortunately, there was a general downturn in the national economy in 1967, including a 61-day strike in the automotive industry that resulted in the cancellation of large advertising campaigns by two Beaumont auto dealers.[10]

Another holding of the diversified Essex Corporation was its stock in Liberty National Bank. Because John also owned personal shares of stock in Liberty, he was heavily involved in management decisions of its board of directors. Under the aggressive management of president Harvey Everest and executive vice president Morrison Tucker, Liberty had grown dramatically both in total deposits and market share in Oklahoma City. However, by spring of 1967, the national economic downturn began to be reflected in Liberty's profitability—a result of substantial charge-offs on loans, lower total deposits, increased overhead costs, and the commencement of the Liberty Credit Card operations.

At the same time, Harvey Everest announced his retirement as president and CEO of Liberty. John and John Kirkpatrick went to San Francisco, California, to interview J.W. "Bill" McLean, a native of Muskogee, Oklahoma, who at the time was director of marketing for the Bank of America in San Francisco. They were pleased with McLean's credentials and recommended him to replace Everest.

Under McLean's direction, by the end of 1967, Liberty had expanded to the point where its most pressing need was space. Recognizing the need to sell the old building before constructing a new one, bank officials quickly went to work to find a buyer.

John's solution was to create Liberty Properties, Ltd., in June, 1968. It was a wholly-owned subsidiary of Liberty Corporation, which was part of Essex Corporation. John then put together a pool of investors for Liberty Properties to purchase the old Liberty Bank Building, which was sold and renamed City National Bank Tower. Eventually, Essex's interest in Liberty was reorganized into Palomar Financial Corporation.

The downturn in value of Liberty National Bank stock put Essex Corporation into a financial squeeze by the summer of 1967. Although Essex held positive assets in Liberty and the Pasteur Medical Building, these assets had been heavily leveraged to secure capital to launch Essex's European and African ventures. With the decrease in Liberty's stock, Essex needed to reorganize.

On July 20, 1967, the stockholders of Essex exchanged all assets and related liabilities of KBMT-TV, Liberty National Bank & Trust Company stock, and the Pasteur Medical Building Corporation for 481,830 shares of common stock in Liberty Corporation, a newly-organized subsidiary, with a value of $1 per share. Half of the Liberty Corporation stock, totaling 240,915 shares, was distributed at a ratio of one-half share of Liberty Corporation per one share of Essex Corporation.

The reorganization divided Essex Corporation's activities into two categories. Essex remained actively engaged in the procurement and sale of oil and natural gas equipment in Europe, the Middle East, and Africa. Likewise, it became a holding company, which owned Liberty Corporation.

Another major change in corporate structure was necessary because of the growing political instability in the Middle East. By 1967, Libya was producing 2.5 million barrels of crude per day, making it the world's seventh largest producer and placing it among the Middle Eastern oil giants. However, looking to the future, Libyan officials wanted Libyans trained to replace foreign oil field workers.

Libyan law provided that whenever a visa for a foreign technician was issued, the oil company bringing that technician had to designate a Libyan who would be trained to replace him. At the same time, King Idris' ministers demanded that foreign oil companies increase both production and exploration for new discoveries. Any future Libyan venture appeared to be very risky.[11]

Also, there was much opposition inside Libya to King Idris because of his refusal to support the Arabs in the 1968 Arab-Israel war. A majority of Libyans believed that Idris and the ruling class were keeping most of the oil revenues while the rest of the population endured horrible poverty. The monarchies of Egypt and Iraq had recently been overthrown, and by August, 1969, rumors of plots and coups were rampant in Libya.

When George Daley approached John in the early summer of 1969 and offered to purchase Sahara Oilfield Services, Trans-Africa Engineering Services, and Essply Limited, John agreed. Because the name Essex was internationally recognized in the oil business, Daley wanted to maintain the name and in exchange was willing to leave some $4.5 million in tax write-offs with the stockholders of the old Essex Corporation.

The sale was consummated on August 15, 1969, just days before Mu'ammar Abu Minyar al-Kadhafi overthrew King Idris on September 1, 1969. By 1973, Kadhafi had totally nationalized some companies and gave the government controlling interests in the remaining ones. Fellow oil men were impressed with John's reading of the Libyan situation, even though he claimed that he did not foresee the revolution and that the timing of the sale was pure luck.[12]

At the time of the sale, John reorganized the assets that Daley did not purchase into a new Okay Corporation. Owners of the 531,830 shares outstanding in Essex Corporation were given three choices. They could sell their old Essex

Corporation stock for $4.61 per share; transfer their old Essex stock for stock in the new Essex Corporation; or trade old Essex stock for stock in Okay Corporation.

The new Okay Corporation, despite all the book assets and the subsidiaries it held, was little more than a hollow shell with a negative net worth. In fact, the negative net worth was Okay's major asset, making it attractive to investors. As the subsidiaries were liquidated, Okay realized a tax write-off of more than $4.5 million. The loss could be carried forward and used when profits were generated so that no taxes were owed on those profits.

Four generations of the Nichols family. Left to right, John W. Nichols; his grandmother, May Tutt Nichols; his father, John T. Nichols; and daughter, Betty. Standing in front is son, Larry Nichols.

twelve

A Family Affair

I doted on the children—but tried not to spoil them.
JOHN W. NICHOLS

J *ohn worked long hours* building his successful and diversified investment business. He often met potential investors for an early breakfast and worked most days until 6:00 p.m. at the office. He also was away from home at least several days each month, looking at new oil properties or visiting with investors. But when John was home, he spent as much time as possible with Mary and the children.

While the children were in school, Mary was an active member of the Oklahoma City Junior League and school-related organizations. She also was a Girl Scout leader, volunteered at Children's Hospital, and taught Sunday school. Larry, Betty, and Kent went to Nichols Hills Elementary School and Casady School, an Episcopal private school in Oklahoma City.

Religion was a major part of the Nichols' life. Each of the children was baptized and confirmed at Oklahoma City's First

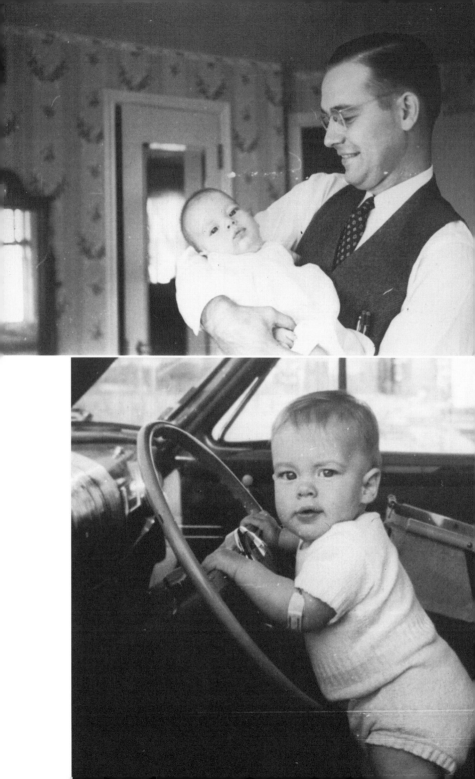

ABOVE: Larry, left, and Betty Ann Nichols, on her first birthday. Betty was born November 23, 1944, at St. Anthony Hospital in Oklahoma City. She weighed six pounds five ounces.

ABOVE LEFT: John holds his first son, John Larry Nichols, born July 6, 1942, in Oklahoma City.

LEFT: A first driving lesson for Larry Nichols.

James Kent Nichols was born October 5, 1949, in Oklahoma City.

Larry, right, and Betty
were John and Mary
Nichols' first two children.

Presbyterian Church, where they regularly attended Sunday
school and church.

John doted on his children, but not to the extent of spoiling
them. When he came home from trips, there were no special
presents. All three children learned quickly that John and Mary
worked together in providing discipline. There was no asking
permission from one and, if turned down, going to the other.

When the children grew old enough to date, they had a rigid curfew.

Holidays were a time of special fun at the Nichols' home. At Halloween, the children loved to dress in costumes and trick or treat. Thanksgiving meant turkey, dressing, and all the trimmings

RIGHT: The mothers and children of the Nichols' Oklahoma City neighborhood in the winter of 1945. Mary is standing at right. Larry is waving from his vantage point on the right front of the sleigh that was pulled by a truck owned by neighbor Barney Stuart. The sleigh was made by A.J. Bullard.

BELOW: Gladys Sparks, who worked for the Nichols for 18 years, was a great help with the children, especially on vacation trips. Left to right, Kent, Gladys, Mary, Betty, and Larry.

at a "big family dinner." Christmas was a special time for the children. The holiday officially began with a big Christmas Eve dinner. Following the meal was the tradition of hanging stockings with the expectation that the next morning they would be filled.

On Christmas morning, the children would get up and dress rather formally, then have breakfast upstairs. They could not

Mary Nichols, right, and Barbara Smith check Junior League files, looking for volunteers to participate in Junior League programs. Mary was very active in several civic organizations and in activities of her children.

come downstairs until grandmother and grandfather Nichols arrived. At the appointed time, the children descended the stairs in order—Kent, the youngest first, then Betty, and finally Larry. After opening their presents, the noon feast was served.[1]

The Nichols loved to travel. Somehow John made time in the summers to take long vacations. John and Mary set out to show their children the world. Before they were out of high school, Larry, Betty, and Kent had been in every state except Maine and Idaho.

John and one-year-old Kent in 1950.

RIGHT: Kent "reading" the newspaper at Christmas, 1951.

Betty Ann Nichols with her baby dolls at Christmas, 1947.

Mary Nichols shows off her catch during a family vacation at Gull Lake, Minnesota, in 1950.

ABOVE: Mary and Betty Nichols.

The three Nichols children in January, 1952. Left to right, Larry, Betty, and Kent.

John with Kent, left, and Betty in front of the Nichols' Christmas tree in 1951.

The Nichols vacationed in Hawaii in 1954. Left to right, Betty, Larry, Mary, and John.

They also spent vacation time in Bermuda and Mexico. In later summers, the family stayed as long as two months in exotic locations in Europe, Libya, Egypt, and Nigeria. The travel broadened the children's horizons and introduced them to different cultures around the globe.

Beginning in the 1940s, John and Mary rented houses on the beach at Long Beach, California, for the summer. They later rented beach houses farther south in Newport Beach and eventually purchased a house on the ocean at Three Arch Bay in Laguna Beach. But how they bought the house is the "rest of the story."

Mary, left, and John T. Nichols, in October, 1951.

John had always wanted to buy a beach house, but when he and brother-in-law, Jim Davis, looked at properties each summer, John always thought they were overpriced.

In January, 1968, a real estate agent called John to try to interest him in one of three different California beach houses. John was scheduled to make a business trip to Japan and consented to stop over in Los Angeles to look at the houses even though he did not intend to buy one of them.

The real estate agent picked John and Mary up at Los Angeles International Airport at 9:00 p.m. one night and quickly showed the three houses. Mary echoed John's feelings when she said, "I don't want to buy a house." John thought that one house was terribly overpriced and told the broker, "I might give 60 percent of that price." John went on to Japan and Mary stayed with her brother in California.

When John returned to the United States, Mary told him, "You bought a house." The owner had accepted John's 60 percent offer. John and Mary knew so little about the house, they disagreed about the entrance—did you walk up or walk down to enter the front door? After all, they had only seen the house once, in the dark. They were both wrong about the entrance—it was level.

The children spent part of many summers at camp. Larry and Kent went to either Camp Lincoln in Minnesota; Cheley Camp in Estes Park, Colorado; or Frontier Ranch in Buena Vista, Colorado. Betty was sent to Camp Waldemar in the Hill Country of Texas, where she later was a counselor. Intermingled with summer camp and the beach were short excursions to national parks, museums, and historic sites, especially during spring vacations.

In 1960, Larry graduated from high school and departed for Princeton University in New Jersey, where he studied geology. He graduated from Princeton in the spring of 1964 and enrolled in the University of Michigan School of Law in Ann Arbor, Michigan.

John and the family dog, Cocoa.

After law school, he served as a law clerk to Justice Tom Clark and Chief Justice Earl Warren of the United States Supreme Court.[2]

During the time Larry worked at the

ABOVE: Larry Nichols at his first formal date at the Oklahoma City Golf and Country Club in 1954. His companion for the evening was Laura Parrish.

Supreme Court, John was involved in several Libyan investments. On a visit to America, John's 51 percent Libyan partner, Kamal Seradge, wanted to visit the Supreme Court. John telephoned Larry who made arrangements for John and Seradge to visit Chief Justice Warren.

At the appointed time, John and Seradge were ushered into the Chief Justice's chambers. When Chief Justice Warren entered, he quickly identified John, whom he had never met, walked up to him, and said, "John, how are you? So good to see you," as if they were longtime friends. Naturally, Seradge was impressed—so was John.[3]

LEFT: John and Mary took their children everywhere. At a Delta Tau Delta convention in Pasadena, California, Metropolitan Opera star James Melton wanted to sing "The Surrey With the Fringe on Top" to some small child from Oklahoma. Someone pointed out that Betty Nichols was a six-year Oklahoman. Melton called Betty to the stage and sang to her. However, in all the excitement, Betty went to sleep in his arms.

ABOVE: John W.'s parents, John T. Nichols and Mary Whiteman Nichols on their 50th wedding anniversary in June, 1955. Joining the celebration are their grandsons, Larry, standing by his grandmother, and Kent.

Betty was in the
seventh grade in 1957.

Larry's ninth grade
photograph in 1957.

The Nichols family at
Christmas, 1956. Left to
right, Larry, Mary, John, Kent,
and Betty. Christmas was a
special time for the family.

RIGHT: Kent was in
the second grade at
Nichols Hills Elementary
School in 1955.

ABOVE: Larry Nichols graduated from Casady High School in Oklahoma City in 1960.

LEFT: A family reunion at Thanksgiving, 1956. Front row, left to right, Jimmy Richard and Kent Nichols. Second row, Mary Lynn Milner, Nancy Richard, Betty Nichols, Mildred Richard, and Clarine Whiteman. Third row, Belle Richard, Will Whiteman, Lillian Simpson, Mary Whiteman Nichols, and John Tutt Nichols. Back row, Bill Whiteman, Charles Richard, Larry Nichols, Mary Nichols, Wayne Milner, and Addie Lee Milner. Seated on the lap of Clarine Whiteman is Mary Lynn Milner.

LEFT: John exploring the underwater world off Bermuda at Shelly Bay in 1955. The Nichols took world-class vacations with their children.

RIGHT: Mary and John on vacation in Italy in 1966.

BELOW: John on vacation at Disneyland in 1960. Left to right, nephew Randy Davis, son Kent, daughter Betty, and John.

ABOVE: John and Mary enjoyed attending parties and special occasions at the Oklahoma City Golf and Country Club.

LEFT: John and Mary always loved to dance.

John and Mary celebrated at a joint birthday party in 1961. He was 47 and she was 45.

In the summer of 1968, Larry joined the Office of Legal Counsel in the Attorney General's office where he worked for Assistant Attorney General William Rehnquist, who later became Chief Justice of the Supreme Court.[4]

Larry fully intended to practice law after his stint at the Justice Department. It was commonplace for former Supreme Court clerks and Justice Department lawyers to join elite Washington law firms. He was still single and believed that he could enjoy the practice of law and participate in the unique lifestyle presented in the nation's capital.[5]

Larry interviewed with some of the top firms in Washington, D.C., including the firm of Oklahoma City native W. DeVier Pierson. However, while waiting to hear from the firms, Larry received an offer from his father to join his company in Oklahoma City.

At first, Larry was hesitant about returning to Oklahoma City. He really wanted to practice law and had been away from his hometown for a decade. He also was contemplating marriage to Polly Ann Puckett of McAlester, Oklahoma, whom he had dated for nearly four years. Polly worked for the Library of Congress.[6]

Larry reached what he thought was a logical decision—try the job with his father in Oklahoma for two years. If it did not work out, he would at least have received some practical business experience and could still practice law in Washington, D.C., or anywhere.[7]

Kent Nichols in the backyard of the Nichols' home at 7300 Nichols Road in Oklahoma City in 1966.

It was a busy year for Larry. He accepted his father's invitation and worked for the company a few months in Denver, Colorado, under the supervision of Kenny Riggs, before returning to Oklahoma City.

He also proposed marriage to Polly. She accepted and they were married on October 16, 1971. Larry had a new job, a wife, and the rigors of establishing a new home in Oklahoma City.[8]

Larry and Polly's first child, a son named John Tyler Nichols, was born on December 31, 1972. Two years later, on September 17, 1974, they became the parents of a daughter, Sally Ann Nichols.[9]

Betty attended kindergarten through sixth grade at Nichols Hills Grade School, then moved on to Casady School. At Casady, she was a cheerleader and was involved in numerous extracurricular activities. By her senior year she had decided to follow in the footsteps of her mother and attend Randolph-Macon Woman's College in Lynchburg, Virginia, where she enrolled in 1962.

Although she did not know it, Betty already had met the man she eventually would marry, David Hargett Street, one of her childhood friends. As babies, they had lived on the same street in Nichols Hills.[10] Both families were members of the First Presbyterian Church.[11]

In 1949, the Street family moved to Colorado Springs, Colorado, where they lived for 10 years before returning to Oklahoma City. In 1961, David enrolled at the University of Oklahoma. About the time Betty went off to college, Mary Nichols and David's mother conspired to get the two together. Neither Betty nor David was enthusiastic about the arranged courtship and David never telephoned.[12]

However, the parents persisted. Finally, during Christmas vacation of 1965, David called, giving in to his mother's request.

When he took Betty on a date, he found out she "wasn't so bad after all."[13]

When Betty and David began dating regularly, she was in her senior year at Randolph-Macon, and he already had graduated from the University of Oklahoma. Because David had enrolled in ROTC at OU, he had incurred a two-year obligation for active duty with the Army. After graduation, he was sent to Army infantry school and military intelligence school. David and Betty were engaged in April, 1966.

He was scheduled for shipment to Vietnam, but his orders were changed. In October, 1966, before he was to report to his new stateside assignment at Fort Lewis in Tacoma, Washington, David was given a two-week furlough, and he suggested to Betty that they get married.[14]

Betty asked her mother which of the two weekends of David's furlough was better? Mary, who along with John were big OU football fans, replied, "If you have your wedding the second weekend, no one is going to come, including me, because that's the day of the OU-Texas football game." So Betty and David were married in Oklahoma City's First Presbyterian Church on October 1, 1966. For the next year and three months Betty "was an Army bride."[15]

Betty and David's first child, Elizabeth Ann Street, was born on October 12, 1967, in Tacoma, Washington.

After his military commitment was fulfilled, David completed his master's degree in business administration at the Wharton School of Business at the University of Pennsylvania.

A son, Randall Hargett "Randy" Street, was born on May 31, 1970, in Philadelphia, Pennsylvania. The Streets' third child, Jeffrey David Street, was born in Princeton, New Jersey, on January 18, 1973.[16]

Even before David completed his MBA in the spring of 1970, his father-in-law, John, suggested that if he wanted to get into the banking business in Oklahoma, a place could be found for him at Liberty Bank. David considered John's offer and another made by John's close friend Morrison Tucker, the chief executive officer of a five-bank consortium in Oklahoma City. However, in June, 1970, David accepted a full-time position with Simulated Environments Inc., a company that produced computer systems to train bank trust departments. David later

John, right, and his "little girl," Betty, at a Christmas dance at the Oklahoma City Golf and Country Club in 1964. Betty made her Oklahoma City debut in 1965 at the Beaux Arts Ball.

ABOVE: Betty, left, and Mary pose in front of a castle on a family vacation to Europe in 1964.

joined his brother in organizing an investment banking company, Street and Street Inc., in New York City.

In 1973, David accepted a position with the First National Bank of Chicago's regional loan office in Kansas City, Missouri. After a few months, he was transferred to the bank's office in San Francisco.[17]

Betty was president of her children's local parent teachers association and worked hard to defeat Proposition 13 in California elections in 1978. She believed the proposition would diminish the quality of public schools. When the proposition passed on June 6, she welcomed David's decision three days later to move from California to Greenwich, Connecticut, where David went to work for Bangor Punta, a manufacturing conglomerate.

She had graduated from the University of Washington and was still in Seattle. Kent quickly wrote back to say, "I am coming to Seattle for a job. . .Let's get together." The reunion resulted in a blossoming romance.[21]

Kent had an opportunity to join NBC in Burbank, California, in a talent job, but instead chose the advertising sales side of broadcasting. He moved to Tucson, Arizona, and became an advertising salesman at KHOS-Radio in early 1975. Shortly thereafter, Diane moved to Tucson and worked at a television station. She and Kent dated for more than a year and were married on May 22, 1976. They were blessed with three daughters during the next few years—Holly Allen Nichols, born in Tucson December 4, 1978; Laurie Ann Nichols, born in Denver, Colorado, November 21, 1982; and Kelly Lynn Nichols, born in Denver March 21, 1984.

Kent quickly developed a reputation for being a marketing expert in broadcasting, rather than simply a broadcaster selling advertising. He saw his job as not to just sell advertising, but to pull people through the front door of a business and move a product off the shelf. He made radio ads visual by creating a "theater of the mind" for the product. This allowed those hearing the message to build their own image of what the product looked like—radio drew the outline and the consumer added the color.[22]

Kent moved to KAIR-Radio in Tucson in 1976 and became national sales manager. The company had both an AM and FM outlet, although the FM station soon changed its call letters to KJYK. Kent's creativity brought him much success in developing new accounts and creating innovative ways to promote both the radio stations and their advertising customers.[23]

When the owner of KAIR and KJYK announced the stations were for sale, Kent was interested. He believed the sales price

After a decade in Connecticut, David went to work for Penn Central, and the family moved to Cincinnati, Ohio. He transferred to General Cable Corporation in 1992 when it was spun off from the giant company. General Cable manufactured insulated wire and cable goods for use in consumer and automotive products. When General Cable was sold in June, 1994, David retired. He and Betty eventually split their living time between Keystone, Colorado, and Atlanta, Georgia.[18]

Kent met his future wife, Diane Elizabeth Hubbard, at Frontier Ranch in Buena Vista, Colorado, when he was 16 and she was 14. The two remained in touch for almost a decade, and then Diane's father, an Edmond, Oklahoma, physician, moved to Seattle, Washington, when she was a freshman at the University of Oklahoma. In the meantime, Kent graduated from Casady School in 1968 and enrolled at the University of Denver in Colorado.[19]

Kent was a pre-med major his first two years of college, but eventually discovered his future was in broadcasting and changed his major to mass communications. He graduated in 1973.

Even before his official graduation ceremony at the University of Denver, Kent took a job at KBMT-TV in Beaumont, Texas. He worked as promotions director and photo-journalist, and served as the station's graphic artist, afternoon movie emcee, and the late night weatherman. He once did a story on hurricane hunters and flew into the eye of a hurricane with them. His stories on Brooks Henley, a mass murderer, were used nationally on the ABC evening news.[20]

In 1974, Kent took a position with ABC News and was assigned to its Denver office. He was caught by the recession and his job was eliminated four months later. At about the same time he began looking for a broadcasting job in the Seattle, Washington, area, he received a Christmas card from Diane.

was a good deal and telephoned his father for advice and financial help. After hearing Kent's ideas, John agreed, and Surrey Broadcasting Company was formed to hold ownership of the two stations.[24]

As president of Surrey Broadcasting, Kent analyzed every facet of the image and programming of the two stations. With changes in format and the consolidation of two sales departments into one, he showed a profit at the stations within a year.

To allow the stations to stay in touch with consumers, Kent established Surrey Research, a marketing research and consulting company. His two Tucson stations were too small to fully support Surrey Research, so its research capabilities also were offered to other media outlets. Surrey was the first broadcasting company to get into the research business and offer it to other broadcasters.[25]

Kent began looking for other broadcasting properties in California, Missouri, and Wisconsin. Within the industry, his reputation was that he was someone who could take a station that was losing money and turn it around in a short time. In late 1980, he found such a property in his hometown of Oklahoma City. KATT-FM had been losing money for some time and was in foreclosure. In June, 1981, Surrey Broadcasting's purchase of the station was approved by the Federal Communications Commission.

Within a few months, Kent and his management team made a profit at KATT-FM which became a leader in the Oklahoma City market. To determine the station's image, he used focus groups with listeners to change their perception of "The Katt." He wanted listeners to perceive that KATT was the best station in town, even though it might not be their favorite station.[26]

As further proof of the success of Surrey management, the company's two stations in Tucson were sold later in 1981 for $5.5, several times their original purchase price.[27]

Later, Kent was joined by his brother and sister in forming Caribou Communications, which purchased Surrey Broadcasting. Other partners were John's longtime friends Cal Stuckeman and Peter Grunebaum. Caribou acquired three other Oklahoma City stations, KYIS-FM, KTNT-FM, and KNTL-FM.[28]

Kent's success with Caribou caught the attention of the executives of Finova, a New York-based finance company, which had sold KYIS-FM to Caribou. Kent and Caribou managers were hired to operate stations that Finova had foreclosed on in Hawaii. Within a short time, the stations had been forged into an attractive cluster of broadcast properties.

Surrey Research was sold in 1988 and renamed Paragon Research; however, Kent retained all rights to the methodology. He continued to conduct his own market research, focus groups, telephone studies, and music tests to make sure that the radio stations maximized their programming and advertising revenue potential. Such attention to detail enabled Caribou Communications to remain a profitable leader in its markets.

By 1999, WWLS-Radio in Oklahoma City, "The Sports Animal," had been added to Caribou's holdings. Kent's two decades of developing proven methods of rescuing money-losing broadcast stations were rewarded in December, 1999, when he sold Caribou to Citadel Broadcasting Company for $62 million. With a strict non-compete clause in the sales agreement, Kent left broadcasting and moved with Diane to Jackson Hole, Wyoming.[29]

Larry and Polly with their first child, John Tyler Nichols, born in Oklahoma City on December 31, 1972.

thirteen

A New Name

What a team! John was the accelerator—Larry was the brake. With both, you had a beautiful car.

MARY NICHOLS

By the late 1960s, John's business interests had become complicated and convoluted. His assets were scattered among numerous businesses, none involving oil and gas exploration and production.

He was convinced gas prices would soon escalate, especially because it appeared that government regulations that had suppressed the exploration for natural gas were changing. His many contacts with European investors had given him an understanding of their investment objectives. While he thought they would be uncomfortable with the risk of drilling exploratory wells, he was convinced they would be interested in buying producing properties in the United States.

To make his idea a reality, John needed new investors and some additional help. He only had four and one-half employees—his secretary, an accountant, two bookkeepers, and a receptionist he shared with another company.

ABOVE: The Nichols family in 1969. Left to right, Kent, Mary, John, Betty, and Larry.

John's first step was to persuade his son, Larry, not to continue his law career in Washington, D.C., but to return to Oklahoma City and help him start their new venture.

John was excited about Larry joining him in the family business, even though Larry would have been justified to ask himself if he had made the right career move. They were starting with one of John's companies that had just sold all of its assets, but had a tax loss carry-forward of nearly $5 million. It had no oil or gas assets.

BELOW: Larry married Polly Ann Puckett October 16, 1971.

Sally Ann Nichols, left, was born in Oklahoma City September 17, 1974. Here she poses with her brother, Tyler.

Larry was exactly what his father was looking for—someone with a legal and geologic background—with no ability to read a financial statement. As Larry said later, "No one who could read a financial statement would have taken the job."[1]

By beginning their business relationship with a new company, John and Larry avoided many potential father-son problems. Because there was no ongoing business, there were no "toes to step on," no long time employees that might be upset if the boss' son rose to the top of the company.

It was just the two of them—John provided the industry savvy and Larry brought legal and geological knowledge. Larry said, "Dad was a great salesman and was completely in charge of raising money. He always saw the big picture." John did not like details—but Larry was a detail man. His legal expertise and affinity for details in putting together a deal was a perfect combination with his father's ability to develop strategy for the new company. Both had mutual respect and confidence in the other's judgment.[2]

Mary saw John and Larry "click" almost immediately. She believed their personalities complemented each other in making decisions. She said, "John was always the dreamer. He could figure out new deals and Larry, often taking a devil's advocate position, could tell him if they would work. John was the accelerator—Larry was the brake. Together, they made a beautiful car."[3]

Larry with kids of the Nichols and Street clan at the beach in 1975.

The only thing the company needed to become a successful oil and gas enterprise was to actually own oil and gas properties. John and Larry were looking for something to buy—and the investors to finance the purchase.

But before John was ready to present his bold future plans to investors, he had to get his corporate structure in working order. He asked his lawyer, Dick Taft, to accompany him to London to meet with a law firm made up of three American lawyers, Ed Gottesman, Sam Evans, and John van Merkensteijn, III, who had studied tax laws of European countries and had become experts in creating legal ways to shelter income and save income taxes for investors.

Van Merkensteijn had been born in Holland but came to America for education at Yale University and the University of Pennsylvania Law School. He had returned to London to practice international tax law where he later became tax adviser to popular music groups such as the Moody Blues.

Taft could not accompany John and Larry to London. He was committed to attend a wedding of a friend's daughter, so he sent young McAfee and Taft lawyer, Gary Fuller, to London. It was the beginning a 30-year close friendship and legal-business partnership between Fuller and the Nichols.

Fuller was already a corporate law veteran, having represented businessman Ross Perot in his early years. Fuller was an original incorporator and lawyer for Perot when Electronic Data Systems (EDS) was created. EDS became one of the nation's most successful computer-age businesses.[4]

Fuller saw some similarities between Perot and John—both had positive attitudes, wonderful senses of humor, and could clearly see long-range plans for their companies.[5]

At a meeting in the London offices of Gottesman, Evans, and van Merkensteijn, John and Larry looked for a new name for a company to hold the assets that remained after the sale of European and African companies to George Daley. The lawyers asked John what he wanted to call the company. Gary Fuller remembered the historic moment:

> Van Merkensteijn was discussing a complicated tax-friendly plan that John could use to attract investors to buy producing oil and gas properties. John had no idea what we would call the company, but he glanced at a map of England on the wall of the law office conference room and started reading off the names of various England counties. When he mentioned Devonshire, Larry said at least that name had some remote tie to the oil and gas business since the Devonian geologic age was named after rocks in that county. That was good enough and they decided that "Devon" would make a good name for the new endeavor. [6]

As soon as Fuller arrived back in Oklahoma City, he began preparing the paperwork for Devon Corporation, officially incorporated as an Oklahoma corporation on February 20, 1970.

Their plan for Devon was to take advantage of existing tax treaties between the United States and several European countries, particularly England, in the same way John earlier had used the American tax code to attract wealthy investors in the United States. John planned to raise money in Europe and use it to acquire oil and gas assets in the United States. Thanks to international treaties, such a relationship would provide substantial tax breaks for European investors.[7]

Fuller and van Merkensteijn created a complicated but effective series of corporations that would attract European investors because of being able to reduce income tax on profits.

The idea was to divide income from a producing property into two main streams—one, a working interest that would produce only a small taxable profit for the company owning the working interest—and second, a royalty income that could be paid to a United Kingdom corporation and be subject only to a maximum 15 percent United States tax. Normally, profit derived by a United States company from oil and gas production in America was subject to the full federal tax.[8]

The Internal Revenue Service would approve the maximum 15 percent tax only if two-thirds of the ownership of the company receiving the royalty was held outside the United States.

To make the plan work, Devon International, S.A. (DI), was incorporated in Luxembourg, as the parent company. Luxembourg was chosen because that country assessed no income tax on corporate profits.[9]

DI directors were Max Lents, co-chairman of Butler, Miller & Lents, Ltd., international petroleum industry consultants; William Waag, director of oil, gas, and mineral investments for the Wall Street investment banking firm of Burnham and Company; Michael "Mike" Robertson; Michael Gellert; London tax and securities attorney Ed Gottesman, van Merkensteijn, Fuller, and Larry.[10]

Coldstream Properties Limited, a wholly-owned subsidiary of DI, was set up as a United Kingdom corporation to receive royalties from production in the United States, subject only to the 15 percent American tax.

Saxon Oil Company, S.A., was a Panamanian corporation that acted as intermediary between DI and the property in the United States because a Luxembourg company could not own real estate abroad. An added benefit was that Saxon avoided tax on principal payments of the production loan from Republic National Bank in Dallas.[11]

Trident Royalty Corporation, wholly owned by DI, was incorporated in Oklahoma and held leases on federal land because United States law would not allow non-American companies to lease federal land.

An English bank was used to collect money from American oil and gas producing properties and pay the money, without the United Kingdom assessing taxes, directly to Devon International in Luxembourg.

Devon Corporation in Oklahoma City, not technically affiliated with Devon International, owned the working interest in properties and was responsible for their operation.

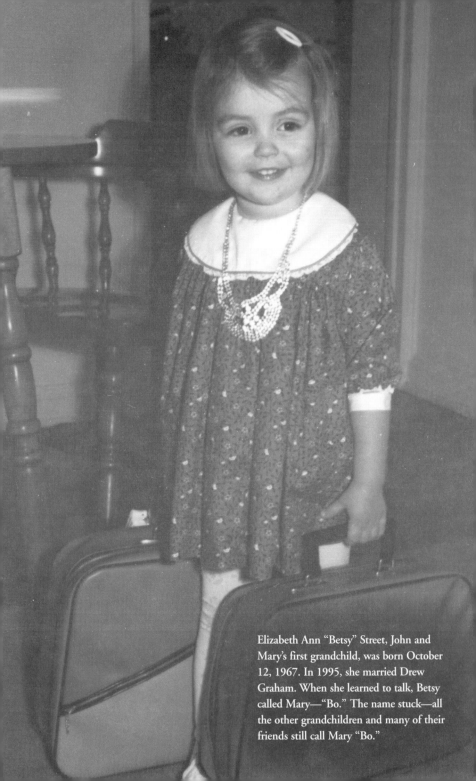

Elizabeth Ann "Betsy" Street, John and Mary's first grandchild, was born October 12, 1967. In 1995, she married Drew Graham. When she learned to talk, Betsy called Mary—"Bo." The name stuck—all the other grandchildren and many of their friends still call Mary "Bo."

fourteen
....

European Investors

John convinced some of the wealthiest investors in Europe to put their money in his risky gas deals in America.

PETER GRUNEBAUM

With legal mechanisms in place, John turned to finding investors for the new enterprise. He had developed a network of friends in key places who could introduce him to other influential people interested in investing in petroleum exploration and production. His business success was well documented, especially in his dealings with some of the world's best-known financiers and oil experts.

Mike Gellert, one of John's friends and an early investor, introduced John to Norman Benzaquen, an investment banker born in Morocco and educated in France and at Columbia University in New York. In 1970, Benzaquen was working for Drexel-Burnham Securities in Paris, France.[1]

Benzaquen, self-described as a civil engineer disguised as a businessman, was immediately impressed with John's ability to explain a petroleum investment deal. Benzaquen said, "John knew how to substantiate an investment. He could sit down with an investor and convince them that he could make good his promises to look for hydrocarbons in the places it most likely existed and that the investor would make more money than in any other available investment."[2]

"John made a market for his ideas," Benzaquen reflected, "Everybody loved him. His accounting background allowed him to chart and explain complicated numbers."[3] Benzaquen would later play a vital role in John's fund raising ventures in Europe.

Another key contact was Peter Grunebaum, a German-born investment banker who became acquainted with John after the wife of one of Grunebaum's friends was impressed with John's explanation of the petroleum business at a cocktail party.[4]

Grunebaum was a veteran international banker by 1970. He was a graduate of Lehigh University and was trained at Chase Manhattan Bank in New York City, at his family bank in Germany, and in Switzerland, London, Buenos Aires, Argentina, and Rio deJaneiro, Brazil.[5]

At first, Grunebaum was skeptical of American oilmen. He was first introduced to the oil and gas business when a Louisiana oilman walked into his New York City office at New York Hanseatic Corporation wearing cowboy boots, a ten gallon hat, and cufflinks that were diamond studded gold drilling rigs. Grunebaum was not impressed with the dreams of the Louisiana promoter and refused to recommend any investment by his clients. Grunebaum's instincts were good—the Louisiana man ended up in jail for defrauding investors within a few years.[6]

John called for an appointment with Grunebaum in New York City. Reluctantly, Grunebaum agreed to listen. "It was love at first sight!" Grunebaum remembered, "John walked into to my office wearing a nice, normal suit and tie. No cowboy boots or ten gallon hats."[7]

"I quickly learned to appreciate John's preparedness," said Grunebaum, "He had a stack of numbers and made me believe that he really could buy oil and gas properties and make a profit for my clients."[8]

Before he could recommend any of John's deals to his list of prominent investors, Grunebaum checked John's references at the Republic National Bank in Dallas. First, Grunebaum called Nick Roberts, head of the bond department at Republic, and asked about John's history. Roberts checked with Ed Montique in the bank's energy department and reported to Grunebaum, "Nichols owes us a couple of million dollars but he's good for whatever he wants. In fact, we'll loan him much more if he wants it."[9]

Grunebaum also checked out John with the help of Fidelifacts, a New York City investigation firm made up of ex-FBI agents. Investigator Tom Norton reported back to Grunebaum a week later. Norton said, "The guy has a great reputation in Oklahoma City. He pays his bills. He's nice. We could find nothing but two lawsuits with the IRS, and Nichols won both of them. His wife is named Mary and he has three children. He's squeaky clean."[10]

Grunebaum was sold on John's integrity and sales ability. He stood ready to help John raise money when the time was right. In fact, in raising money for John's oil and gas deals, Grunebaum never had a written agreement with John—they simply trusted each other.

Although he accepted John's concept, Grunebaum had some misgivings about introducing John to sophisticated European bankers. Grunebaum thought John had the worst Oklahoma accent he had ever heard. He also believed that John's visit to

ABOVE: David Street, left, and Betsy Street.

RIGHT: Betty Nichols Street and her children, left to right, Betsy; Jeffrey David Street, born January 18, 1973; and Randall Hargett "Randy" Street, born May 31, 1970.

New York City had probably been the only time he had been outside of Oklahoma. Grunebaum was terrified by the thought that, "John would show up in Europe in a maroon jacket and plaid trousers and white shoes."[11]

However, when Grunebaum and John met for breakfast at London's Savoy Hotel, John appeared wearing a dark blue suit, black shoes, and a white shirt. Grunebaum breathed a sigh of relief. As the two men climbed into a cab, John asked, "Where is our first meeting?" Grunebaum told him it was at Guinnes-Mahon, a centuries-old European bank. When John told the cab

LEFT: Mary and grandson, Randy Street.

BELOW: The grinning three Nichols grandsons. Left to right, Jeffrey Street, Tyler Nichols, and Randy Street.

driver what route to take, Grunebaum began to suspect that John was more than he had first appeared. John later revealed to his new London friend that he lived in the city for six months during previous business ventures and knew the sprawling city well.[12]

With a briefcase full of paperwork, John and Grunebaum presented the plan to officials at Guinness-Mahon. If bank officials saw a problem, the ever-optimistic John would say, "That's a hurdle we can get over. I'll take care of it."[13] The bank was interested and wanted John to assure them that his lawyers could make certain that securities used for collateral would be issued in Luxembourg.

John presented to bank's concern to van Merkensteijn, who said, "Come back in four days. I'll have something drafted." After meetings with other banks in London, Grunebaum and John went to Paris to meet with officials of the Bank of Suez. John continued to impress Grunebaum with his knowledge of foreign cities.[14]

With exploratory talks with bankers and financiers completed, Grunebaum and John returned to London to see van Merkensteijn's draft of a memorandum for a Euro-dollar offering. However, an impasse developed over the precise language in the memorandum.

To speed up the process, John asked Fuller to catch the next flight to London. Once in England, Fuller quickly worked out details of the offering.[15]

To please Guinness-Mahon, John needed a stack of legal documents from his Oklahoma City office. He could not wait weeks for the paperwork to arrive by mail so he asked his assistant, Norma Wade, to pack the paperwork in a suitcase and immediately fly to London.

With a commitment from Guinness-Mahon in hand, Grunebaum and John flew to Berlin, Germany, to meet with potential investors. From Berlin, they traveled to Cologne, Germany, to present the plan to Peter Wehahn, head of two huge German companies, and the patriarch of one of Germany's most prominent Catholic families. The Wehahn family controlled ABC Bank, one of the country's largest financial institutions. Peter Wehahn was so impressed with John's frank presentation of the oil and gas investment scheme, he committed to be an investor on the spot.

For many years, John and Wehahn were dear friends. It was not uncommon for John to attend Wehahn's birthday celebrations. One year, Wehahn told John by telephone that he was having a birthday party the next night. John made immediate plans and flew to Germany. When Wehahn died in 2001, he bequeathed John nearly $500,000, with the provision that he give the money to his favorite charity. Wehahn, a lifelong devout Catholic, further limited any gifts to churches to Catholic churches. John complied with his late friend's wishes and made substantial contributions to universities, including the University of Oklahoma and Randolph-Macon Woman's College.[16]

Norman Benzaquen led John to other major European investors. Sofina was a huge holding company in Brussels, Belgium, that invested in Devon drilling programs. Leo Deschyteneer was a high executive in Sofina who became good friends with John. In a typical funding package, investors would put up two million dollars and Devon took a percentage of the deal for putting it together.[17]

One of the most famous of Devon's European investors was Prince Albert Von Oettinger Spielberg of the Bavarian royal family in Germany. On one occasion John and Benzaquen visited the family castle outside Munich where extensive remodeling was taking place. John mentioned that he and Mary were remodeling their house in Oklahoma City less than ten years after it was built. John asked the prince when his house was built. The prince replied, "Oh, about 900 years ago."[18]

Now that investors were identified, all that was lacking was an oil and gas property—Devon needed to actually buy producing oil and gas properties.

Larry and John found a potential property in the Currie Field in Navarro County, Texas. McCormick Oil Company owned five producing natural gas wells and some of the investors in the company wanted to sell. With natural gas selling at 16 cents per MCF, Devon believed the investment could generate a good profit. At the very least, the purchase of a minority interest in the five McCormick properties for approximately $2 million would give Devon a portfolio of oil and gas properties on which to build the future.[19]

Devon borrowed $1 million and found investors for the remaining $1 million to complete the McCormick purchase. John was able to sell investors on the deal because of intricate production reports and pro formas prepared by Larry, with the help of a computer program developed by attorney Reford Bond.

While Gary Fuller and John were in Europe raising money, Larry was in the United States investigating the properties and preparing computer projections that showed how cash would flow through the various corporations back to European investors. Because business application for computers was in its infancy, Devon did not own its own computer, but had to use a time-shared computer that was only available at night.

One evening, as John and Fuller were completing a meeting with investors in London, an investor sent Larry a Telex asking a few questions about the property. It was 2:00 a.m. in Oklahoma City, and the investor did not expect an answer until the following day. However, Larry was working on the time-share computer and responded in a few minutes, causing the investor to ask John how he had persuaded Larry to install a Telex machine at his bedside.

One night while Larry was working at the computer, he thought he heard something in the hallway outside his office. When he opened the stairwell door to take a peek, the door slammed behind him, locking him out of his office. Larry had to walk in stocking feet from his office on the 33rd floor of the Liberty National Bank Building.

His assistant, Susan Ketch, one of Devon's first employees, remembered, "He had blisters and much pain for a few days." For the next few nights thereafter, Ketch left the office each night with the admonition to Larry, "Be sure to keep your shoes on tonight!"[20]

Money was tight in the early days of Devon. When Ketch considered taking another job that paid just $25 a month more, Larry said there was no money in the budget to match the offer. However, Ketch stayed at Devon. She recalled, "Larry talked me out of leaving. He said it the company failed, he could practice law and would give me a job." Ketch is among many Devon workers who described the Nichols as "generous" to their employees.[21]

The Devon team was off and running. The money was raised to finance the McCormick purchase and Devon finally owned oil and gas properties. Devon's future looked bright.

John and Mary accompanied nine other Oklahoma City couples on a trip to the Arctic Ocean in the summer of 1974. In this photograph, they rest on a pile of rocks at the Arctic Circle. During the trip, they traveled to Banks Island—only 150 miles from the North Pole.

fifteen

A Partnership with P&O

*John would always say, "Fuller, let's just do the deal
and we'll paper it up later."*

ATTORNEY GARY FULLER

J ohn's concept for funding his acquisition program was simple.
Devon International would make a semi-public offer-
ing to the Peninsular and Oriental Steam Navigation
Company (P & O) and other select European investors.
Devon Corporation would then invest the funds in oil and
gas properties in the United States.

P & O was a healthy financial partner. The company was
founded in 1815 in England and was the world's largest shipping company. P & O, in its first 100 years, was the world's
leading mail carrier, applying the technology ushered in by
the Industrial Revolution to bring frequency and regularity to
international communications.[1]

P & O was responsible for the word "posh" in the English
language that described upscale accommodations. When rich

passengers sailed the P & O to India, they asked for the best cabins, P.O.S.H., or portside out starboard home, because of the prevailing winds that helped cool non-air conditioned cabins.

John made contact with P & O because of his business relationship with Mike Robertson, called "Lord Huntley" by Larry because of Robertson's formal English name of Huntley-Robertson.

How the contact was made is ironic. Robertson's secretary, Ann Symonds, knew Michael K. "Mike" Taylor, a British-born petroleum engineer and graduate of the Royal School of Mines in London, whose father had worked for P & O for four decades. Taylor, known as "Mr. Oil" at P & O, was manager of oil and gas exploration and was in charge of the shipping company's recent ventures into oil and gas production in the North Sea. Petroleum exploration and production was a new area for P & O that for a century and a half had concentrated on carrying freight and passengers and running a fleet of tankers and ferries.[2]

After John made his presentation to Taylor about P & O becoming Devon's partner in American oil and gas production, Taylor thought the complicated scheme was "crazy."[3] However, he consented to a second meeting with John and Robertson. After that meeting, Taylor began to understand John's plan—P & O would actually loan money to Devon to purchase oil and gas properties, make money off interest on the loan, and receive a share of royalties when the properties produced.

Taylor knew John was a recognized expert and could sell potential investors with his "Gee Whiz, it's a good deal!" presentation. However, even though Taylor was becoming a believer in John's dream, he seriously doubted if the P & O board would approve the multi-million dollar investment with Devon. Taylor reported to his boss, A.B. "Sandy" Marshall, head of bulk shipping for P & O. In a report dated May 5, 1972, Taylor recognized P & O's need for immediate profit and suggested that the company acquire oil and gas producing properties in the United States. Taylor recommended P & O join forces with Devon, primarily based upon John's successful 20-year track record.[4]

In November, 1972, John met with several P & O directors to solidify the deal. John was persuasive with the "formidable" board that consisted of two lords and several sirs. Michael Taylor made the formal presentation of the proposed P & O involvement because his cohort, Jim Lindars, who was scheduled to make the presentation, was stuck in a London train tunnel.[5]

The P & O board listened carefully and voted overwhelmingly to risk millions on the promises of the conservative dressed oilman from Oklahoma City, John Nichols. The lone dissenting vote came from Sir Andrew Matland-McGill-Crichton, who thought it unwise to invest in any American scheme.[6]

John personally negotiated many subsequent contracts with P & O. Taylor said, "John was the greatest entrepreneur I ever met." John's success at negotiation may have been grounded in the fact that he truly conveyed his belief that he could walk away from any deal. He sometimes said, "I don't need this deal." When he arose from his chair and started toward the door, negotiators across the table often folded and agreed to John's terms.[7]

Once, after days of dealing with the bureaucracy of P & O, John threatened to leave the bargaining table. He said, "I've got to go to Dallas, Texas, because I have an appointment with 22 men." What his British counterparts did not know was that John's appointment was with the 22 starting players at the annual Oklahoma-Texas football game at the Cotton Bowl.[8]

With P & O on board as a major partner of Devon's operations in America, it became much easier to find European investors. From that point on, a pattern of operation developed—once Larry located the potential property, John would fly to Europe to raise money to develop the lease. In fact, John was in London so often that he thought about buying a flat. How the Nichols flat in London became a reality is another one of those "accidents" in John's life.

At a meeting of the Randolph-Macon Woman's College Board of Trustees, the chairman announced a $15 million capital campaign and told fellow trustees that the campaign would not go forward unless half the money, $7.5 million, was raised at that meeting. The chairman went around the table, asking each member, "What are you going to do?"

John had a quick idea. When the chairman looked his way, John said, "I'll give the college money to buy a flat in London. It could be available for use by substantial contributors to the capital campaign." John explained that he also would be able to use the flat during his lifetime. The Board of Trustees liked the idea.

After consulting with Mary, a two-bedroom, two-bath flat was purchased in a building in the central part of the city, just a three or four minute walk from Harrods, the legendary department store, and within easy distance of Hyde Park.[9]

On the long flights between Europe and America John often struck up conversations with fellow passengers. Once, as he was flying the trans-Atlantic Concorde, John began talking with the person sitting beside him, an Englishman. Almost naturally the conservation turned to banks and banking. When his fellow traveler mentioned an act of the Bank of England with which John disagreed, John pointedly told him that the Bank of England had no idea what it was doing and its policies were idiotic. As the Concorde landed, John and the Englishman exchanged business cards. When John looked at the one he had received, it read, "Gordon Richardson, Governor of the Bank of England."[10]

On another flight, the man seated next to John discovered that he was in the petroleum business and a long discussion followed. John noticed that the female flight attendants were "really pampering" his fellow traveler, but thought nothing of it. He heard the passenger being called "Mr. Redford," but that meant nothing to him.

When they were landing, the passenger asked if John had a business card. John asked, "By the way, Mr. Redford. What business are you in?" Robert Redford said, "I like guys like you. I'm in entertainment." When John arrived home he called Larry and asked, "Do know a guy named Robert Redford, who says he's in entertainment?" Larry told his father about Redford and his latest movie, "Butch Cassidy and the Sundance Kid." John thereafter made a special effort to see Redford's movies and later telephoned him to compliment him on his work.[11]

Flying the Atlantic was not a costly proposition for John. He took advantage of a one-time offer to buy a lifetime pass on American Airlines for $25,000. That purchase turned out to be one of John's best investments. By 2004, John had flown nearly five million free miles on American. For example, a round trip fare to London was only $28.50, the amount of the airport tax.[12]

In 1973, John and Larry learned that Commonwealth Gas Corporation, headquartered in Charleston, West Virginia,

Diane Elizabeth Hubbard Nichols, right, Kent's wife, and her two youngest daughters, left, Laurie Ann Nichols, born November 21, 1982, and Kelly Lynn Nichols, born March 21, 1984.

and Southwest Gas Company, headquartered in Monroe, Louisiana, were for sale. The two companies held producing properties in Wyoming, Louisiana, and West Virginia, as well as some undeveloped leases.

John and Larry jumped at the opportunity because they both agreed that if Devon could acquire the two companies at the right price, it would put Devon solidly in the black.[13]

Commonwealth Gas and Southwest Gas both were owned by Isabelle Ferrington of New York City. Larry immediately began analyzing the assets and negotiating an acquisition contract. At the same time, John began work on the financing with Devon International's European investors.

Larry spent months in New York City negotiating with Ferrington's agents. Each night, he reported to John on the day's negotiations. Larry was very intent on crafting a deal Devon could "live with," but John's advice was, "All that sounds fine Larry, but don't lose the deal!"[14]

Devon's main hurdle was that no one wanted to invest money in the project until they knew they owned the field— and Ferrington did not want to sell until she was sure John and Larry had enough money.[15]

Just when John and Larry thought the negotiations were successfully concluded, Ferrington wanted a performance guarantee. To satisfy the demand, John and Larry turned to the Oklahoma-based Eason Oil and Gas Company. They told Eason CEO Winston Eason that if Eason would provide Devon with a financial cover, Eason could have 50 percent of the transaction at closing for half the cost. A second part of the proposal was that if Devon could not come up with its half of the purchase price, Eason could have the whole deal.[16]

Eason officials agreed and provided the financial backing to satisfy Ferrington. Then, John raised most of the purchase price of $26 million for Commonwealth Gas and Southwest Gas from P & O.

Larry and McAfee and Taft lawyer, Reford Bond, negotiated with Ferrington's attorneys in New York City for several more months. Finally, Larry told Mrs. Ferrington that he was not bluffing, but that his wife was about to give birth to a baby and he was going home to Oklahoma for a long time. Mrs. Ferrington used the news to prompt her lawyers to quickly finish the deal.[17]

After the final documents were prepared, Larry and Bond planned to have dinner with Mrs. Ferrington at the University Club in Manhattan. While they waited, one of Ferrington's lawyers approached them with a grim face, announcing there was one last issue that had to be resolved. Fortunately, the "one issue" was a request that Mrs. Ferrington be given a new set of tires for her company car she was keeping. Larry and Bond pledged to personally buy the tires and put them on that night, if that is what it took to close the deal. Larry remembered, "We weren't going to blow a $26 million deal over a set of tires."[18]

While P & O was the lead investor, John and Mike Robertson visited more than 100 merchant or investment banks in Europe looking for remaining funds necessary to close the deal. They often visited a half-dozen banks a day.

Robertson described John's presentation to bankers, "John had one helluva brain. He was focused on his mission—to convince potential investors that he knew what he was doing. He was not flamboyant—but quietly sold them on his dreams." Robertson trusted John implicitly and had no

Grandpa John with Holly Allen Nichols, born December 4, 1978, the first child of Kent and Diane Nichols.

problem recommending John's deals to his colleagues in the petroleum industry.[19]

Everywhere Robertson traveled, he tried to sell participation in Devon's ventures. Once, he sold shares to a man he met on a ski slop in Norway.[20]

The money for drilling in Wyoming, Louisiana, and West Virginia, the most risky part of the Commonwealth and Southwest investment, came from a partnership with the family that owned the Smedvig Shipping Company of Stavanger, Norway.

It was Robertson's contacts that allowed Devon to join forces with Smedvig. Robertson had a friend who worked for SEDCO, the Texas drilling firm founded by later Texas Governor William Clements. SEDCO had a strong relationship with Smedvig, giving Robertson the opportunity to take John to a meeting with Harald Johansen, the chief assistant to Torolf Smedwig, the founder of the huge company.[21]

After an initial meeting with Johansen, John was invited to return to Norway on several occasions before Smedvig agreed to invest in Devon's projects. On one occasion, attorney Reford Bond accompanied John. When Smedvig discovered that Bond, a Choctaw Indian from Oklahoma, was an expert in Norse mythology, he was truly impressed. John had to wait for hours listening to Norse stories before he could get back to selling his oil and gas ideas.

Not only did the Devon-Smedvig partnership allow exploratory drilling on the newly acquired property, it also produced a close personal friendship between Larry Nichols and Peter Smedvig, the son of the wealthy owner of the company. In 2004, Larry still served on the Smedvig board of directors.[22]

It took three days in a windowless room in the basement of a Bermuda hotel to sign documents necessary to complete the Commonwealth-Southwest acquisition. Many of the documents required two witnesses, so attorney Gary Fuller and Larry took their wives. However, they failed to explain to them how long the closing would take. The two wives arrived on the first day in their tennis outfits, not knowing they would spend three days in the basement of the hotel.[23]

After the closing, John, Mike Taylor, and others returned home, leaving Larry and Fuller and their wives to vacation for a few days. All hotel accounts were transferred to Larry's name to handle when he left. When Larry and Fuller prepared to check out, they discovered the hotel in Bermuda did not accept credit cards or non-Bermuda checks. Larry had to call upon Devon's Bermuda attorney to pay the hotel bill so they could leave.[24]

With the Commonwealth-Southwest acquisition, Devon followed two strategies—buying properties that were producing and drilling for new production. The producing properties, which Devon owned 50-50 with Eason Oil Company, were "bread-and-butter" operations in a field with a long history. Thus, there was neither a tremendous amount of risk in drilling nor a high dollar return. The Commonwealth holdings also included an intrastate gas pipeline, which collected gas from almost all its wells and transported it to a small group of industrial customers in Huntington, West Virginia.[25]

The Devon-Eason partnership operated the leases for a decade until Eason executives offered to sell their shares in 1983. Larry liked the idea because Devon's interest could double without increased overhead. Devon offered Eason more than $10 million for the West Virginia leases.

At first Eason officials agreed, but then the price of oil soared to $40 per barrel, with some oil analysts predicting $100-a-barrel oil. Between 1980 and 1983, an estimated $2 billion per year flowed into production income funds from investors hoping to cash in on the boom. The strategy of production income funds was to buy production and then wait for $100-a-barrel oil. So, when a production income fund offered Eason $18 million for its share of the field it jointly owned with Devon, Eason officials balked at the $10 million deal with Devon.[26]

When Larry and John looked at the $18 million offer, they agreed that it was absurd. The production of the West Virginia wells was not sufficient to make such a purchase economically sound. So rather than buy Eason's share, John and Larry decided to sell Devon's West Virginia holdings to the same income fund. The deal was made and both John and Larry believed they received far more than the interest was worth.[27]

This was not the only time Devon followed what was described as a "contrarian philosophy," making decisions opposite of the conventional wisdom in the oil business. In 1978, for example, Devon paid $5.2 million for 37,000 acres of undeveloped acreage, two-thirds of which was in the Deep Anadarko Basin of western Oklahoma.

At the time, the Deep Anadarko was called the greatest new natural gas field in the history of the petroleum industry. The problem was that producing zones were more than 20,000 feet deep—expensive to reach. However, when federal regulators deregulated the price of natural gas below 15,000 feet in the early 1980s, prices jumped to nearly $10 per MCF. Oil men were in a frenzy and the cost of leases in the Deep Anadarko rocketed to incredible prices.[28]

Larry and John looked at the situation and realized there was more money to be made by selling—than drilling. The acreage that Devon had bought for approximately $141 per acre was sold for as much as $5,280 per acre, plus a 50 percent backing on each well drilled on the property. That meant Devon would receive half the net profit—and none of the risk—if a company drilled a successful well. It was a smart decision because five of the six companies that bought Devon property in the Deep Anadarko went bankrupt when the boom went bust.

In June, 1974, John proposed that P & O finance the purchase of two Louisiana companies founded by John E. Fowler, Jr. of Shreveport. Falco, Inc. transported crude oil in its 38 transport trucks and owned 80 miles of pipeline in Arkansas and Louisiana. The company had a terminal in Jonesville, Louisiana, where crude was loaded onto barges on the Ouachita River for transport to the Mississippi River and the Gulf of Mexico.

Falco and a sister company, J.E. Fowler Petroleum Products, Inc., purchased nearly a million barrels of crude each month from oil producers in Louisiana, Arkansas, Texas, and Florida.

John and Mike Taylor convinced the P & O board to underwrite the $9 million purchase of the two Louisiana transportation corporations that were merged into Falco Holding Company. After the closing in Shreveport, Taylor left for London with $3 million in negotiable securities in the briefcase. Needless to say, he did not sleep on the long flight to London.[29]

In 1974, Devon either operated or participated in the drilling of 33 exploratory test wells and 11 development wells. As a result, by the end of April, 1975, the company had made one major discovery in Nebraska, acquired potential productive leases in both Colorado and Oklahoma, and had two successful wildcat completions in West Virginia. As of December 31, 1974, Devon had an interest in 817 producing gas wells and 140 producing oil wells in 10 states.[30]

John carves Mr. Turkey for the family's
1979 Thanksgiving dinner.

sixteen

Major Expansion

*The oil industry is one big family—
no matter who is drilling a hole in the ground,
we are all on the sidelines rooting for him to strike oil.*

JOHN W. NICHOLS

In 1975, Devon acquired Kirby Oil Company. Headquartered in Houston, Texas, and listed on the American Stock Exchange, Kirby Oil was well known in the oil fraternity, with the Murchison family of Dallas among its major shareholders. After negotiations, the purchase price was set at $54,633,000.

All but $2.8 million of the money necessary to fund the Kirby purchase came from P & O and a few other banks, but it was the last few dollars that came hard. For the next two and a half months, John called on 104 investment institutions in both the United States and Europe before he finally persuaded the Ouachita National Bank of Monroe, Louisiana, to put up the last $500,000. A like amount came from the investment firm of Drexel-Burnham.[1]

However, just as the transaction was being closed, a segment of the financing failed. John and Larry were in Houston,

John and Mary used their house on Laguna Beach, California, frequently for vacations and hosting groups of friends and family. Here Dr. Lynn Harrison, left, and attorney Kenneth McAfee play gin rummy.

Texas, closing the transaction. Larry was on one floor of the law firm reviewing the closing documents and concluding some final negotiations, while John was on another floor scrambling "to fill the gap."[2] Several times during the day, Larry received written messages from John that simply said, "Slow down," as he secured the missing money.[3]

Following his father's instructions, Larry would ask an endless stream of questions or request to take one last look at some title opinion or document. By late afternoon, John had made a few calls and found new sources of money to finance the deal. He walked into the room where Larry was and, with a big smile, said, "We can go now."[4]

Kirby added 281 wells, located primarily in Texas, Oklahoma, and Louisiana with more than 18 million barrels of oil reserves, and 55 billion cubic feet of gas reserves to Devon's holdings. Devon operated 275 of the wells, which meant hiring 20 additional people to oversee the operation. By the end of 1975, Devon had interests in oil and gas wells in 13 states and showed a profit for the year of $2,874,000. Three years later, Devon added more gas-producing properties in Oklahoma at a cost in excess of $26 million.

That same year, 1978, there was a major downturn in the shipping industry, forcing both the Smedvig family and P & O to withdraw from Devon's investment projects. The

John continued his support of college fraternities long after his graduation from OU. He attended the 50th anniversary celebration of the Intrafraternity Council in Stillwater. Left to right, OSU president, Dr. Robert Kamm; attorney Burns Hargis; John; United States Supreme Court Justice Tom Clark; Dr. Jim Struthers, pastor of Stillwater's First Presbyterian Church; Dr. Frank McFarland; and Dave Pickrell.

Kirby acquisition was the last partnership between P & O and Devon. P & O management changed and the British shipping giant decided to cease all oil and gas investments. In dividing the assets acquired with P & O, Devon received 20 percent of the holdings. As Michael Taylor saw it, "John got away with the goods."[5]

During negotiations to split Falco's holdings, P & O officials came to Oklahoma City and offered Devon very little of the Falco assets. John, Larry, and attorney Gary Fuller held fast to their position and negotiated a wonderful arrangement in which P & O took Falco's transportation and marketing portfolio and Devon was able to rid itself of a huge debt.[6]

The split-up of Falco, a move called by Fuller "the divorce with P & O," was a significant event in the life of Devon. The deal made Devon debt-free, no doubt a major factor is allowing Devon to survive during the next few years when the petroleum industry bust drove many debt-laden companies into bankruptcy.[7]

After Michael Taylor left P & O, John invested in Taylor's 1977 attempt to raise the *San Jose*, a Spanish ship that had sunk two centuries before off the coast of Columbia. It was rumored that the ship contained $600 million of treasure. John was the largest investor in the plan to salvage the ship. Taylor put together the technical team to raise the ship, but could never obtain the cooperation of the Columbian government.[8]

As always, John came up with creative methods in finding replacement funds. In the last quarter of 1978, Devon closed its first public drilling program, which raised $5 million through Merrill, Lynch, Pierce, Fenner & Smith, Inc. The money was used to drill 30 wells, 20 of them producers and 10 dry holes. A second drilling program was sold in 1979 for $10 million, funding the drilling of 45 wells, with 11 of them producing oil and gas.

In all there were five drilling funds sold through Merrill, Lynch, Pierce, Fenner & Smith between 1978 and 1982. In each, Devon served as the general partner of limited partnerships and received 40 percent of the revenue generated in return for paying all capitalized costs. In addition, Devon received a management fee for each of the programs.[9]

Although profitable, the arrangement did not satisfy the investment firm that wanted larger funds than Devon was willing to participate in. Even so, John and Larry refused to compromise their conservative policy.

In addition to the drilling funds with Merrill Lynch, John and Larry established new partnerships with new European investors to buy producing properties. In 1979, with $26 million from two new partnerships, the company purchased 173 producing wells in the Arkoma Basin of southeastern Oklahoma. Other acquisitions included Shawnee Oil and Gas for $11.7 million in 1980; Carson Petroleum for $13 million, also in 1980; and Cominco American in 1982 for $31 million.

Also in 1982, members of the royal family of Kuwait purchased 12 percent ownership of Devon for $16 million. The deal was brokered by Scottish management consultant Thomas Fenton "Tom" Ferguson, a delightful man who represented Sheik Nasser and two of his siblings of the Al-Sabah family. Ferguson, operating from his office in London, was looking for an American oil and gas investment when Peter Grunebaum introduced him to John.[10]

Ferguson, who became a member of Devon's board of directors in 1982, and continued to serve in 2004, chose Devon in which to invest his clients' money because of the integrity he observed. Ferguson said, "The straightforwardness of everyone from the head of the company to the newest employee was evident. There was a family ethic atmosphere. They were a bunch of nice, smart, honest folks!"[11]

John's cosmopolitan view of the world also convinced Ferguson that Devon was the right choice for investment. Ferguson shared a common European view that people living in America's Midwest were not terribly interested in world affairs—but he knew John and Larry were different.[12]

All of Devon's expansion came when the price of oil was high. At the time of the Shawnee acquisition, for example, the price of oil was $35 a barrel. In projecting what would happen in the future, conservative experts thought the price would stay flat at $35 a barrel, but Larry believed that the price would fall as low as $30 or even $27 a barrel. "We impressed our investors as well as ourselves at how conservative we were," Larry later said. Despite the conservative outlook, however, neither Larry nor John foresaw the dramatic bust that was to come.[13]

The boom ended in the mid-1980s in a collapse that sent the oil industry spiraling. Historians W. David Baird and Danney Goble wrote:

> The oil bubble burst. The OPEC nations broke rank, and world oil prices began a mad retreat. Oklahoma oilmen gave up their dreams of forty and fifty dollars a barrel. Instead they suffered nightmares as crude prices slipped down an oily slope...In a matter of weeks crude

prices fell from $27 to $13…Car dealers took back their fancy cars, their metallic gold paint covered with Oklahoma's unforgiving red mud.[14]

Petroleum prices tumbled to less than $10 a barrel and natural gas prices declined precipitously, but Devon was not hurt as seriously as other independent producers. John and Larry knew the time for selling public drilling funds for limited partnerships had passed, and in May, 1985, the five that had been sold were merged into a master partnership named Devon Resource Investors, which was traded on the American Stock Exchange. This allowed liquidity for the investors who already had received the tax benefits they had been seeking. The new arrangement also allowed Devon to manage one entity rather than five, a "win-win situation."[15]

Devon remained a low-cost operator, which enabled it to avoid layoffs and maintain a clean financial statement. Even so, 1986 was a "hunker down" year in production. For the next year and a half, Devon followed its conservative pattern of a deliberate, low-risk drilling program to increase reserves but not unduly risk great financial losses.[16]

During this time, John and Larry began to formulate plans for Devon's future. By 1987 they were managing several entities—Devon Resource Investors, an old drilling fund with the Smedvigs; three production acquisition partnerships with various Europeans; and Devon Corporation. Since 1979, the number of shareholders in Devon, because of deaths and divided inheritances, had grown to more than 200, making Devon technically a widely held private company, but yet not really public.

Larry urged John either to dispose of the multiple holdings and become a truly private company, which would end the duplicated cost of running several companies, or merge them under the umbrella of one large public company. By eliminating the partnership arrangements and going public, it would allow them to raise more money for investments.

As they analyzed the situation, John and Larry predicted that major oil and gas companies would continue to be international and that independent energy companies would continue to consolidate. Acting on that prediction, they decided to combine all operations into one public corporation. The creation of the new entity, to be known as Devon Energy Corporation, meant that the net worth of each part of the old partnerships and companies had to be assessed.

It required a vote by everyone holding shares in each of the old entities. The merger was ultimately approved by 100 percent of the private partners and 99.2 percent of the shares held in Devon Resource Investors.

The transition was smooth. In September, 1988, the stock in Devon Resource Investors halted trading one day—the next day Devon Energy Corporation began trading as a public corporation. There was no initial public offering and the entire change was made without litigation. Devon Energy originally was incorporated under the laws of Delaware, but registered as an Oklahoma corporation in 1995. Its assets included reserves of 5.84 million barrels of oil and more than 67.2 billion cubic feet of natural gas.[17]

John was named chairman of the board and Larry became president and chief executive officer of Devon Energy Corporation. John continued to travel the United States and Europe to keep shareholders aware of what was happening to the company and what to expect in the future. His status as chairman of the board of Devon freed him from much of the work of running the company. John maintained separate offices in the Mid-America Tower and had his own staff of employees. Also, he continued to oversee the Lillian Simpson Trust and remained a partner and operator of FHN and managed his personally owned leases and royalties in Oklahoma, Texas, New Mexico, and Mississippi. He devoted much of his time to civic and philanthropic endeavors as well as to family and travel.

John went searching for his ancestral roots in 1983. In this photograph, he stands in front of the Grace Episcopal Church in St. Francesville, Louisiana. The church is one of Louisiana's oldest Protestant congregations. John's ancestors are buried in the adjacent cemetery.

seventeen
. . . .

Devon Energy

A public vehicle is a much more efficient way to raise capital.
LARRY NICHOLS

Devon Energy became a major player in the national energy industry during the final two decades of the 20th century. Larry continued to oversee Devon's growth using the two-pronged approach in which he and his father believed—acquisition of producing production and drilling for new discoveries. Between 1987 and 1993, Devon made 12 acquisitions involving more than 7,000 wells. Among them were leases in the Permian Basin of West Texas, southeastern New Mexico, and the San Juan Basin of northwest New Mexico.[1]

Initially developed by Blackwood & Nichols in the early 1950s, numerous gas wells had been drilled in the Northeast Blanco Unit in northwest New Mexico on 320-acre spacing. Their production was sold to El Paso Natural Gas (El Paso) on a 20-year contract for approximately 15 cents per MCF. Charles Blackwood managed the property, overseeing maintenance of the wells, collecting payments for the gas sold, and making distributions to his partners—John, Bill and Helen Hilseweck, and John Fisher.

Under the provisions of the Federal Natural Gas Act, when Blackwood & Nichols' contract with El Paso expired in 1972, the company was required to continue to sell its output to the gas utility at the old contract price. For the sale to be terminated, Blackwood & Nichols had to receive an abandonment order from the Federal Power Commission.

The price for natural gas had risen from 15 cents per MCF to 30 to 40 cents per MCF since the original 20-year contract had been negotiated. A new contract would at least double the price. There was no incentive for El Paso to negotiate, a position that was hardened by Blackwood & Nichols' refusal to allow a price reduction when the cost of natural gas had fallen in the late 1950s.

John held lengthy discussions with his attorneys, Terry Barrett and Stan Cunningham, who told him that he could make a unilateral rate change and then try to justify it before the Federal Power Commission (FPC), a move that was time-consuming and expensive. And, the FPC, bowing to political pressure, was dedicated to keeping natural gas prices low.

John's other option was to file a lawsuit with the FPC, alleging that El Paso was not negotiating in good faith. John decided to sue. Blackwood & Nichols filed an action with the FPC designed to get maximum publicity. El Paso officials were undaunted and adopted a hard line attitude.[2]

As the price for natural gas soared to as high as $2.75 per MCF, producers claimed their overrides should be based on that price rather than the price at the time the contracts were negotiated. El Paso naturally disagreed. The result was a lawsuit by producers such as Blackwood & Nichols.

El Paso responded by filing a complaint against all the producers with the Federal Power Commission, arguing that the contracts were tantamount to an actual sale of the gas, as opposed to an override. El Paso maintained that the override payment should be based on a price of 51 cents per MCF rather than $2.75.[3]

Blackwood & Nichols was one of more than 70 producers sued by El Paso. When the case was heard by a federal judge in Washington, D.C., the courtroom was crowded with dozens of lawyers representing the various producers. Each company put on witnesses and the hearing was "drawn out until everyone's nerves were frayed."[4]

When it came time for attorney Terry Barrett to present the case for Blackwood & Nichols, he put John on the stand. All previous witnesses had talked about the contracts that had been executed by El Paso and some deceased former official of their companies. One witness said, "My father signed the deal."

The federal judge was delighted to learn that John was the only witness who actually had participated in the original negotiations. He provided information that no one else could have and greatly impressed the judge. When it came time for opposing lawyers to cross examine John, they announced, "We have no questions." The judge was shocked. He said, "What do you mean, you have no questions? The judge looked at John and said, "Well, I do. We've had hearings for six weeks and this is the only man who really knows about the original contract."[5]

When El Paso lost the case, it refused to wire the money to Oklahoma City, perhaps wanting to draw interest on it as long as possible. John personally flew to El Paso, Texas, picked up the $25 million check, and wondered how he was going to cash the instrument drawn on a tiny bank in New Jersey. For an answer, he called officials at Republic National Bank in Dallas.[6]

The bank suggested the check needed to be presented at the Federal Reserve Bank in Philadelphia. John met a bank official in Dallas who flew to Philadelphia and hand-delivered the check. Before midnight, the $25 million was available.

By the 1980s, the way of doing business for Devon was far different than in the 1950s—especially the travel involved. In the 1950s, John might take a train to Chicago, spend the night, take another train to New York City, and then spend three or four weeks raising money, going to plays at night. In the 1980s, Larry often made a breakfast presentation in one Merrill Lynch office in the morning, fly to the next city for a lunch presentation, fly to still another city for a late afternoon meeting, drive across town for a dinner presentation, and fly to another city to repeat the routine the following day.[7]

After two or three weeks of being on the road, Larry, on more than one occasion, emerged from an office building, sur-

LEFT: John was a supporter of the Oklahoma City Zoo. He and Mary gave money in 1982 to fund the Dromedary camel exhibit.

RIGHT: In 1980, John was awarded an honorary Ph.D. in Business Administration by Bethany College in Bethany, Virginia.

Mary relaxes a moment during a 1980 vacation in the Smoky Mountains.

veyed the parking lot, and had absolutely no idea what color or kind of car he had rented.[8]

In 1988, Larry saw an opportunity to go back into the San Juan Basin, thanks to Section 29 of the Tax Act of 1986. As Oil Producing and Exporting Countries

(OPEC) was draining hundreds of billions of dollars out of the United States for petroleum purchases, the federal government was looking for alternate and new sources of energy. One such alternative was producing natural gas from coal deposits. Section 29 called for a federal subsidy for what was known as coal seam gas, a subsidy that began at 83 cents per MCF and later rose to $1.00 per MCF. The subsidy originally was scheduled to expire in 2000 but later was extended to 2002.

However, there were problems associated with recovering gas from coal deposits. The most significant problem was the amount of water that came to the surface with the gas. Blackwood & Nichols wells in the Northeast Blanco in the early 1950s had been drilled through seams of coal, known as the Fruitland, which averaged 50 to 60 feet in thick at an average depth of 3,000 feet. At the time, John realized that gas could be produced from the coal seams, but the large amount of water associated with it made production of the gas uneconomical. Consequently, the gas was cased off as wells were drilled through to a much deeper producing zone to large deposits of natural gas.[9]

With the enactment of Section 29, Amoco and Meridian, and several other companies with holdings in the San Juan Basin, began tests to determine if there was coal seam gas present. The conventional geological wisdom was that a normal well first would produce oil and/or gas and then, as it was pumped, the amount of water gradually would increase in the output.

Petroleum engineers had developed a curve that predicted when the output of water would increase—and the output of oil and/or gas would decrease to the point where the well no longer was profitable. When that point the reached, the well was capped.[10]

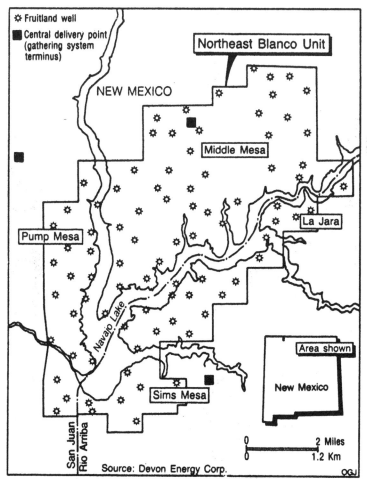

Devon Energy Corporation stepped up its drilling of wells in the Northeast Blanco Unit in 1988 to remove gas from coal seams deep beneath the earth. *Courtesy Devon Energy Corporation.*

With coal seam gas, however, the petroleum engineers found the curve worked in reverse. First, there was a high output of water with a small amount of gas adhering to the water molecules. But as production continued, the amount of water diminished and the gas increased. Larry followed the developments closely, and in 1988, decided Devon should take a strong position in its Northeast Blanco Unit.[11]

In order to drill into the Fruitland and begin producing coal seam gas, Devon invested $20 million of the $90 million total cost of the project. Devon had to purchase rights to drill in the 32,000-acre Northeast Blanco Unit from Amoco, Phillips, Conoco, Northwest Pipeline, Meridian, and several other companies.[12]

Devon then negotiated with Charles Blackwood for a farm-out of the Blackwood & Nichols interest. Once negotiations were concluded, Devon moved forward in what would prove to be the new public company's first big project. Devon would have to drill 102 wells, build 162 miles of pipeline to gather the water and dispose of it, and gather the gas and take it to a central point where the carbon dioxide could be removed.[13]

The process would take three years before any natural gas would be available for sale. It was a huge gamble, Larry realized, for an independent oil company to wait so long for cash flow to start. However, Larry was confident the project would be successful.[14]

With Mike Lacey overseeing the project, as vice president for operations, and Mack Duckworth serving as manager of operations and engineering, Devon drilled 102 coal seam wells on 320-acre spacing to an average depth of 3,000 feet, with an average drilling and completion cost of $400,000 per well. There were significant additional expenses associated with the project. For example, the water that came to the surface with the gas contained particles of coal and other chemicals. The disposal required huge storage and settling tanks, separators, and injection wells because of Environmental Protection Agency standards, adding another $6 million to the total cost.[15]

Larry's prediction was correct. The project was completed and ultimately proved to be very profitable. The coal seam gas was marketed by El Paso Natural Gas, which served California and the Gulf Coast, and by Northwest Pipeline, which transported gas to Washington and Oregon.

With the success of the coal seam gas exploration behind him, Larry discovered that financing of new acquisitions became easier. Because Devon had increased its reserves by 500 percent and its production by 40 percent in 1988, potential investors were encouraged.

There were two reasons why Larry led the discussion to take Devon Energy public in 1988. He was convinced that gas prices would ultimately rise beyond present levels and that there would be massive consolidation among the more than 400 public oil and gas companies in America. From its founding, Devon had been acquisition oriented and had developed a smooth and effective process for finding, evaluating, and acquiring companies. The investors in Devon's projects agreed to go public, and Larry's prediction that America's publicly-traded oil and gas companies would consolidate was right on target. In the next 15 years, Devon would complete more than 100 acquisitions.[16]

Gary Fuller prepared paperwork to incorporate Devon Energy Corporation as a Delaware corporation. On August 10, 1989, Devon began trading publicly on the American Stock Exchange. Within two weeks, the $25-per-share public offering of 1.2 million shares of newly issued convertible preferred stock was closed. Devon finance vice president William Vaughn told a newspaper reporter that the stock offering had given the company more financial flexibility.[17]

In 1990, Devon's bottom line increased dramatically because of continuing federal tax credits resulting from the coal seam gas exploration and production.

By 1991, *The Oil and Gas Journal* ranked Devon as 102nd in total assets among independent oil and gas firms based in the United States.[18]

Mary and John at Christmas, 1980.

In May, 1982, John and Mary and friends visited the Culzean Castle in Scotland. Front row, left to right, Mrs. John Mott, Ruth Bozalis, Mary, Eleanor Kirkpatrick, and John Mott. Back row, John Kirkpatrick and George Bozalis.

Mary and John get ready for the day's van excursion on a 1983 trip to England.

John Nichols, left, and Charles Blackwood, the son of Blackie Blackwood, pose at the wellhead of one of John and Blackie's original gas wells in New Mexico.

eighteen

....

Aggressive Expansion

In the future, only a handful of independent oil and
gas producers will focus on production in America.
We want to be part of that exclusive group.

LARRY NICHOLS

In 1992, *Larry oversaw the purchase* of Hondo Oil and Gas
Company, which doubled Devon's total assets and raised its
rank to the nation's 78th largest independent oil and gas producer. Through First Boston Corporation and Smith Barney,
Harris Upham & Company, Devon sold 9.2 million shares of
new stock at $10 per share, netting $86.6 million. Devon then
used bank debt to fund the remainder of the purchase price of
$126.6 million.[1]

The acquisition of Hondo added 13.3 million barrels of oil
and 91.3 billion cubic feet of gas to Devon's proven reserves.
In addition, Devon gained drilling rights to 218,000 acres of
undeveloped leaseholds, mostly in the Permian Basin of West
Texas.

In May, 1994, Alta Energy Corporation stockholders traded their stock for shares in Devon. The merger, which was Devon's 14th major acquisition in 7 years, was valued at $65 million and added reserves of 24.3 million barrels of oil and 26.6 billion cubic feet of natural gas to Devon's holdings. This increased the company's oil reserves by 163 percent and its total oil and gas reserves by almost 40 percent.[2]

Larry's growing stature in the national energy industry was affirmed in January, 1995, when he was elected president of the Domestic Petroleum Council, a national trade association that represented 21 of the nation's largest independent oil and gas companies. Larry played a key role in focusing the organization's efforts on key issues impacting the operations of the member companies.

In 1997, Larry was presented the Leadership Award of the Independent Petroleum Association of America and the Dean A. McGee Award from the Downtown Now organization.

In June, 1995, Devon changed its legal corporate home— changing its state of incorporation from Delaware to Oklahoma. The move saved approximately $150,000 in annual franchise tax.[3]

In November, 1995, Devon paid $51 million for 80 percent of Unocal's interest in the Worland, Five-Mile, and Rattlesnake Creek fields in Wyoming, along with a gas plant there. The acquisition included 90 billion MCF of natural gas and 13,000 acres of undeveloped leases.

By 1996, Devon was one of Oklahoma's fastest growing public companies. For months, Larry and his top advisors worked on a major acquisition of properties owned by oil and gas pioneer Kerr-McGee Corporation in Oklahoma City.

On December 31, 1996, Devon purchased all of Kerr-McGee's North American onshore oil and gas fields for $297 million in stock. Kerr-McGee received 9,954,000 shares of newly issued Devon stock, giving it ownership of approximately 31 percent of Devon. In return, Devon was totally debt free.[4]

Under the agreement Kerr-McGee was allowed to name three of the nine members of Devon's Board of Directors. The agreement also included a "standstill" clause, which limited future purchases of Devon shares by Kerr-McGee. Devon hired 72 Kerr-McGee employees, bringing its work force to more than 300.[5]

The Kerr-McGee acquisition raised Devon's proven reserves to 24 million barrels of oil and 170 billion cubic feet of gas. The added properties increased Devon's proven reserves by approximately 50 percent and tripled the company's inventory of undeveloped properties.

The next trading day after the agreement was announced, Devon stock increased in value by 11 percent on the American Stock Exchange. The Kerr-McGee deal, combined with the successful completion of 190 wells in 1996, caused *The Oil and Gas Journal* to rank Devon as the 53rd largest independent oil and gas company based in the United States. Devon closed out the year with total revenue of $217.9 million and net income of $54.5 million.[6]

Devon spent the ensuing year "digesting" its recent acquisitions and expanding its production. On June 30, 1997, Devon stock closed at $36.75, up from $24.50 one year earlier. Market value of the company was $1.55 billion.[7] In 1997, the company's net earnings doubled to $73.5 million and the firm set a 10th consecutive record for oil and gas production. Drilling and related expenditures topped $100 million, and 284 of 295 wells drilled were completed successfully.[8]

By early 1997, Devon had outgrown the office space it rented in the Mid-America Tower Building. To allow for future expansion, the company purchased the building.

Larry was active as president of the Domestic Petroleum Council, vice president of the Natural Gas Supply Association, and was elected to the board of governors of the American Stock Exchange in 1997.

At every opportunity, Larry warned of the continuing threat of the federal government taking huge chunks of land from oil and gas production or imposing such strict regulations that operators could not economically drill on federal land. He said, "Sooner or later, the country is going to realize that you can

ABOVE: John and Larry had long opposed Devon owning its own aircraft. However, as airline security became questionable in America, the Devon board suggested Larry and company officials fly in private aircraft the company purchased. A Falcon jet, bearing John's initials and the July, 1969, date of Devon's incorporation, became the primary method Larry used to travel around the country. In this photograph, John appears with his CPA, Darla Neuendorf, left, and, Devon executive assistant Ginger Armstrong.

LEFT: In 2002, the Nichols children visited the home in Nichols Hills where they grew up. The house, at 1715 Pennington Way, is now owned by Lee and Suzie Symcox. Left to right, John, Kent, Larry, Betty, and Mary.

restrict and restrict and pretty soon we won't have the oil and gas supply we need."[9]

Larry recognized that when a gas supply crisis someday hit the country, the industry would be blamed. But he said, "When that day happens, my answer will be, 'Don't yell at us, Mr. Senator, because we don't have enough gas and there are people in gasoline lines.'" Larry believed Americans' desire for low natural gas prices was shortsighted and would eventually harm the oil and gas industry upon which they relied to produce low-cost natural gas.[10]

Devon was in an enviable position in 1998 as oil prices plummeted. Because the company was debt free, its program of acquiring additional oil and gas properties continued. While other operators struggled with their bankers, Devon's leadership team looked across the country at low-cost acquisition targets.

On September 28, 1998, *Fortune* Magazine proclaimed Devon to be among "America's Fastest-Growing Companies."[11] Less than three months later, Devon completed its largest deal to date, the acquisition of Canadian-based Northstar Energy Corp. Devon issued 16.1 million common equivalent shares to Northstar shareholders and assumed $312 million of Northstar debt to acquire the $828 million company. Devon then became one of the 15 largest American-based oil and gas producers.[12]

Devon also took steps to assure the long-term viability of its coalseam gas production in Wyoming with the completion of an arrangement with KN Energy Company to jointly invest $110 million in 126 miles of new gathering pipeline in the Powder River Basin. Completed in mid-1999, the project gave the region's producers access to at least four interstate pipelines and made it possible for Devon to develop 160,000 acres of gas-rights in the Gilette, Wyoming, area.

Devon took another giant step in its growth in 1999 with its purchase of PennzEnergy Company. Headquartered in Houston, PennzEnergy formerly was a part of Pennzoil, but had been spun off in December, 1998, when Pennzoil separated its exploration and productions assets from its motor oil, refinery, and fast-change oil business. This created two publicly traded companies-Pennzoil-Quaker State and PennzEnergy.[13]

Devon paid $675 million and assumed $1.59 billion in debt for PennzEnergy. The acquisition, which doubled the size of its reserves, made Devon the eighth largest American-based independent oil and gas exploration and production company. It also increased the number of Devon employees to 1,550 and caused Phillip Pace of Credit Suisse First Boston to upgrade his evaluation of Devon stock from "buy" to "strong buy."[14]

The PennzEnergy acquisition added a number of world-wide holdings, some of which were sold to reduce Devon's debt. In addition, Devon raised another $400 million in capital for debt reduction by the issuance of new shares of Devon stock. A streamlining of duplicate operations resulting from their merger allowed another $50 to $60 million in savings annually.

Larry announced that Devon would continue to headquarter in Oklahoma City with no changes in the company's management structure. A Devon office in Houston managed the company's offshore activities in the Gulf of Mexico.

Another ramification of the PennzEnergy merger was John's retirement as Devon's chairman of the board to allow James L. Pate of PennzEnergy to assume the position. John's new title was chairman emeritus of the board. Larry remained president and chief executive officer with the understanding that he would become chairman of the board upon Pate's retirement.

Devon's dramatic leap into a "major player" in the energy industry soon attracted the attention of the *Wall Street Journal*. In August, 1999, the *Journal* noted that "scrappy Devon," did not focus on looks, but on leadership. The office of Devon's chief executive was always open and Larry was "always was ready to do more deals, if the price is right."[15]

In August, 2000, Devon absorbed Santa Fe Snyder Corporation to climb to the fourth position on the list of independent oil and gas companies in the United States. The merger, which was Devon's largest, cost the company $2.35 billion in stock and the assumption of approximately $1 billion of Santa Fe Snyder's debt and liabilities. Under the agreement, Santa Fe Snyder shareholders received approximately 32 percent of the combined company, while Devon shareholders retained approximately 68 percent. The total market value of Devon's outstanding shares of stock rose to $7.7 billion and the company's debt rating actually was upgraded despite having "ingested" a company nearly as large as itself.[16]

The acquisition also increased Devon's pro forma enterprise value to approximately $9 billion and its proven reserves to 1.1 billion barrels of oil equivalent. Some 76 percent of the company's reserves were in North America and were weighted 58 percent to natural gas. Devon also had additional reserves in Azerbaijan, Southeast Asia, South America, and in the Pearl River Mouth Basin of the South China Sea. As the *Wall Street Journal* reported after the acquisition, "almost as if on cue... natural-gas prices rose to all-time highs."[17]

Soon after the Santa Fe Snyder acquisition, Larry and John were pleasantly surprised to learn that Standard and Poor had decided to add Devon to its prestigious list of 500 leading companies in the United States. The Standard and Poor's 500 companies are the generally the largest and best-managed companies in the nation, based upon the research and judgment of the Standard and Poor company. The announcement came as a complete surprise.[18]

Devon joined four other Oklahoma-based companies in the Standard and Poor's 500—Phillips Petroleum Company; ONEOK, Inc.; Williams; and Kerr-McGee Corporation. Devon's dramatic growth and outstanding management also was recognized by *The Sunday Oklahoman* in its annual "Oklahoma, Inc." on October 15, 2000. Devon was listed as Oklahoma's top company for the year, based on a system that rewards profitable growth.[19]

Devon's acquisitions were good for Oklahoma's economy. After each merger or acquisition, Devon imported jobs to the Sooner State, employing nearly one third of its 1,500 worldwide employees in Oklahoma City.

In the fall of 2000, Devon reported major exploration discoveries on Sumatra and Salawati Island in Indonesia. The company also disclosed progress on a formal agreement to sell natural gas from its Sumatran blocks in Singapore. One offshore Sumatran well, in 105 feet of water, produced more than 900 barrels of oil and 2.5 MCF of natural gas during its early days.[20]

"We're in the business of looking for things to acquire every day of the year, just as we're in the business for places to drill every day of the year," Larry told a reporter during an interview in October, 2000. He said by keeping operating costs low, Devon was able to ride out inevitable busts in the oil and gas business that cycle in the economy every few years.[21]

In May, 2001, Larry reported to Devon shareholders at the company's annual meeting in Oklahoma City. Pointing to a billion-dollar drilling budget, a 64 percent increase in proven reserves, and record earnings of $730 million, Larry predicted a great future for the company.[22]

As the 21st century began, Devon led the way in the race to consolidate oil and gas operations in the nation. As *The Daily*

Oklahoman observed, "Natural gas companies have been selling lately like windshield scrapers during an ice storm."[23] The buying spree continued despite a drop in natural gas prices.

In 2001, Devon announced it was buying two large energy companies for a total of $8.1 billion in cash, stock, and debt assumption. One reason that Larry wanted to buy Canada-based Anderson Exploration Ltd. was a $6 billion credit line at interest rates at or below 4.5 percent. The other large company that Devon had its eye on was Mitchell Energy & Development Corporation, even though it would take awhile to consummate that deal. Mitchell Energy, based in Houston, owned six natural gas processing plants, 9,000 miles of pipeline, and nearly 3,000 undrilled energy sites in north Texas.[24]

In August, 2001, Devon signed an agreement to acquire Mitchell Energy for $3.1 billion and the assumption of $400 million of debt. Devon completed a private placement of 10-year notes and 30-year bonds to finance the purchase of Mitchell and Anderson. The Mitchell acquisition was the tenth major deal engineered by Larry and Devon since 1992. It also was the largest Devon acquisition to date. It gave Devon 2.5 trillion cubic feet of gas reserve. Business analysts called the acquisition "good for both parties."[25]

In February, 2003, Devon merged with Houston-based Ocean Energy Inc. in a $5 billion deal, and became the largest independent oil and natural gas producer in the United States—as well as the continent's largest owner of oil and gas reserves. Devon, with a net worth of $21 billion, also became Oklahoma's largest publicly traded company. Devon was three times larger than the state's most famous oil and gas company, Kerr-McGee Corporation.

Devon's 2003 net earnings of $1.7 billion climbed 1,500 percent, making the year the most profitable in company history.

The company drilled 2,116 successful wells in 2003, a 32 percent increase over the previous year. Producing wells were added in Texas, Canada, Equatorial Guinea, in the Gulf of Mexico, and in the Panyu Field offshore China.

In 2004, Devon produced 2.5 million cubic feet a natural gas per day—behind only British Petroleum and Exxon in that major league of production. Devon produced more gas than Shell and ConocoPhillips. In fact, Devon produced four percent of all natural gas used in America.[26]

The nation's business journals took note of Devon's rise to the top of the natural gas world. Headlines in business magazines read "By Leaps and Bounds" and "Envy of the Industry." One report said Devon had "the Midas touch."[27]

J. Leland Gourley, in his *Friday* newspaper column, summed up the importance of the Devon growth, citing statistics that showed Devon had become larger that Delta Airlines, Eastman Kodak, Nike, Marriott Hotels, Yahoo, Goodyear, Georgia-Pacific, Apple, and Dillards.[28]

Because Devon had acquired Houston-based multi-billion dollar companies four years in a row, it was only fitting that a 36-story building in downtown Houston was renamed "Devon Energy Tower." The name changed after Devon doubled its presence in the building formerly known as Two Allen Center.[29]

The string of acquisitions brought Devon's worldwide employee total from 213 in 1996 to 4,000 in 2004—with 700 top management people in Oklahoma City.

Larry and his father, John, continued to be bullish on Oklahoma City. When other companies, such as ConocoPhillips, were announcing plans to move corporate headquarters to Texas, Larry said, "Oklahoma City has made tremendous strides...our city is just a better place to live."[30]

The original directors of Devon Energy Corporation. Left to right, H.R. Sanders, Jr.; Thomas F. Ferguson; Larry Nichols; John Nichols; David M. Gavrin; and Michael E. Gellert. *Courtesy Devon Energy Corporation.*

INSET LEFT: Left to right, Polly Nichols, Larry Nichols, Tyler Nichols, and Sally Nichols, at a reception honoring Larry as a Distinguished Graduate of Casady School. *Courtesy Oklahoma Publishing Company.*

ABOVE: Campbell Stuckeman was a member of the board of directors of Devon from 1979 to 1993. *Courtesy Devon Energy Corporation.*

LEFT: Larry Nichols oversaw incredible growth of Devon Energy Corporation in the 1990s. As the 21st century began, Devon became the third largest producer of natural gas on the North American continent. *Courtesy Oklahoma Publishing Company.*

LEFT: H.R. Sanders, Jr., became a Devon director in 1981, a year after the company was founded. Sanders had previously been John Nichols' banker at Republic National Bank in Dallas, Texas. *Courtesy Devon Energy Corporation.*

ABOVE: Returning to their production roots, the Nichols family visited the original Blackwood & Nichols unit in Rio Arriba County, New Mexico, in 1990. Left to right, Kent Nichols, Larry Nichols, Mary Nichols, Betty Nichols Street, and John Nichols. *Courtesy Devon Energy Corporation.*

LEFT: The board of directors of Devon Energy Corporation toured the company's production in New Mexico in 1990. Left to right, J.W. McLean of Oklahoma City; Michael E. Gellert of New York City, the longest-serving member of the board; David M. Gavrin of New York City; Larry Nichols; H. Campbell Stuckeman of Pittsburgh, an heir of the Rockwell International fortune; John Nichols; Tom Ferguson of London, representing the Kuwaiti investors; and H. R. Sanders, Jr., former vice president of Republic National Bank of Dallas. *Courtesy Devon Energy Corporation.*

As Larry, right, assumed more control over Devon Energy, John had more time to travel with Mary and increase his activities for his church and worthy charitable and educational causes. *Courtesy Devon Energy Corporation.*

RIGHT: Devon director Thomas F. Ferguson joined the board in 1982, after he made the largest purchase ever of Devon stock. One million shares of Devon stock was sold to Kuwaiti investors for $16 million. *Courtesy Devon Energy Corporation.*

ABOVE: John W. Fisher served on the Devon board of directors from 1983 to 1992. Fisher played an important role in John Nichols' early success in attracting investors to financing oil and gas drilling. *Courtesy Devon Energy Corporation.*

In October, 2000, Devon Energy
Corporation reported initial production
from two new natural gas wells drilled
from this platform on Eugene Island
Block 156 in the Gulf of Mexico.
Courtesy Devon Energy Corporation.

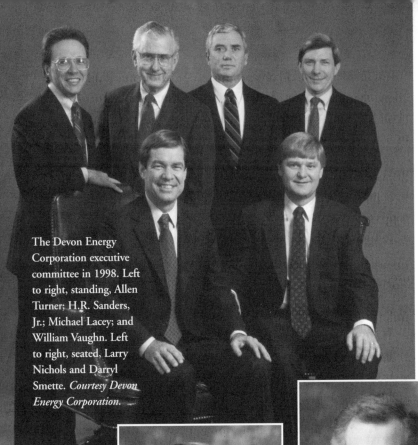

The Devon Energy Corporation executive committee in 1998. Left to right, standing, Allen Turner; H.R. Sanders, Jr.; Michael Lacey; and William Vaughn. Left to right, seated, Larry Nichols and Darryl Smette. *Courtesy Devon Energy Corporation.*

RIGHT: Michael E. Gellert is the longest serving member of the Devon Energy Corporation board of directors. Gellert, a Drexel-Burnham securities dealer who lives in Greenwich, Connecticut, began service on the board on Devon's predecessor company on July 25, 1969. *Courtesy Devon Energy Corporation.*

ABOVE: David M. Gavrin has been a director of Devon Energy Corporation since July 25, 1979. *Courtesy Devon Energy Corporation.*

ABOVE: Grandsons Jeff, left, and Randy Street.

LEFT: Kent and Diane and their three daughters. Left to right, standing, Laurie, Kent, Holly, and Diane. In the wagon is Kelly.

In 2001, John, left, and Mary, right, provided special funding for the John and Mary Nichols Rare Books and Special Collections at the Bizzell Library at the University of Oklahoma. Dean Sul H. Lee, center, led the effort to name the project after the Nichols who are long time supporters of the university library. The collection was founded to promote scholarship in the field of English literature and to provide stewardship for the general collection of rare books within the OU library system. Courtesy University of Oklahoma.

nineteen

Giving Back to Oklahoma

Every worthwhile activity in Oklahoma City—
the arts, opera, music, and theater—have benefited because
of the generosity of John and Mary Nichols.

JACK H. ABERNATHY

O*n November 16, 1987,* John received the highest honor of his native state when he was inducted into the Oklahoma Hall of Fame. Among the other honorees that year was Wal-Mart founder Sam Walton, a native of Kingfisher, Oklahoma.

In nominating John for the Hall of Fame, oilman Jack H. Abernathy wrote, "I cannot accurately estimate the influence on Oklahoma of investment funds that grew from John's original idea in 1949—although in recent years, up to one billion dollars have been spent annually by oil and gas explorers. The fallout in terms of community benefit is incalculable."[1]

Longtime friend John W. Fisher introduced John at the Hall of Fame induction ceremony. Fisher, chairman emeritus of the

John Nichols, right, was inducted into the Oklahoma Hall of Fame in 1987. When Larry was later inducted, the Nichols became only the second father-son team to receive the state's highest honor. The other father-son duo in the Oklahoma Hall of Fame is former Congressman Lyle H. Boren and his son, former Governor, United States Senator, and OU President David L. Boren.

RIGHT: Mary and John Nichols arm-in-arm with the mascot of KATT-FM in Oklahoma City, part of the Nichols' broadcast holdings until its sale in 1999.

BELOW: Mary and John pose with the Hamburg Steinway concert grand piano they gave to the Oklahoma City Philharmonic Orchestra in 1994. Concert pianist Jose Feghali called the instrument one of the two best pianos in the United States. *Courtesy Oklahoma Publishing Company.*

The John W. and Mary D. Nichols Oklahoma Heritage Scholarship is awarded annually by the Oklahoma Heritage Association to an outstanding high school senior. In this photograph are John and Mary with former recipients of the $10,000 scholarship. Left to right, Rebecca Drummond, Ryan McMullen, Mary, John, Aubrey Price, and Luke Bell. *Courtesy Oklahoma Heritage Association.*

Ball Corporation, talked about John's contributions to American petroleum, "When we talk about prominent leaders, we usually list those ingenious inventors who developed the tools we use to find and produce oil. But with John, we have the opportunity to talk about one who had vision to create major new financial structures that have enabled the industry to attract the capital it needs. Without that capital, nothing else would be possible."[2]

John served as president of the Oklahoma Heritage Association in 1991 and 1992. In that capacity, he provided outstanding leadership for the non-profit organization that oversees the Oklahoma Hall of Fame and publishes books and magazines about the Sooner State. Among his contributions to the Association was the establishment of the President's Circle designation to recognize those whose annual membership contributions were $5,000 or higher, and he successfully encouraged a significant number of other companies, foundations, and individuals to join Devon as President's Circle members.

As John turned more and more of the daily management of Devon over to Larry, and with the success of Betty and Kent assured, John and Mary returned to what they loved most in his semi-retirement—travel and family. Voyages along the Norwegian fjords and Inland Waterway of Alaska and trips to St. John's in the Virgin Islands and Cancun in the Yucatan Peninsula of Mexico highlighted family vacations, as did visits to Hawaii, Sicily, and Malta. John especially enjoyed traveling to major golf tournaments such as the Masters and the Ryders Cup.[3]

John was adept at combining his passion for travel with his work. He always believed in keeping his investors fully informed about what was being done with their money, how their wells were doing, trends in the market, and he preferred to do this in person when possible.

During their many travels, Mary began to collect Dorothy Dowdy Birds. Only some 350 to 500 birds of a specific type are issued—making them in great demand. John began buying the birds for Mary whenever he was in London, and as Mary's collection grew, John asked antique dealers in London to be on the lookout for the collectibles.

Gradually, through purchase or surprise gifts from John, Mary had all of both series of Dowdy Birds except one—which gave Larry an idea for a family joke. One day as he was walking by a drugstore, Larry glanced inside and saw garishly colored plastic birds which somehow endlessly dipped their heads to drink. Larry purchased one of the plastic birds and packed it in one of the Dowdy Birds wooden shipping boxes. With the bobbing, eternally drinking plastic bird covered up inside, it looked exactly like the genuine Dowdy Bird needed for Mary to complete her collection. Larry placed the box under the Nichols' Christmas tree with Mary's name on the tag.[4]

Mary was ecstatic and ripped away the wrapping—knowing her long sought Dowdy Bird was inside. She was dumbfounded to find the plastic dipping bird instead. However, her astonishment turned to joy as the entire family burst out laughing.[5]

Mary spent much of her time landscaping their home at 7300 Nichols Road. With great care, she planned the surrounding flowers and shrubbery which was supplemented with seasonal plants from early spring to late autumn.

In his eight-plus decades, John Nichols has maintained a strong sense of duty, lived his faith, not just on Sundays, but seven days a week, and demonstrated civic generosity. Through his life he has been sustained by his absolute faith in God. When asked, he explained, "A lot of people scoff at religion, but for me it works. It really works. I'm a firm believer that you cannot out-give the Lord. I'm certain the Good Lord took care of me."

Because of his strong religious beliefs, he faithfully supported the First Presbyterian Church of Oklahoma City. In addition to giving money, he has served the church as an Elder, on the board of trustees, the building committee, and the finance committee.[6]

The Nichols family faith was tested, like so many other Oklahomans, when they personally experienced the horror of the Oklahoma City bombing on April 19, 1995. At 9:02 that morning, a huge explosion devastated the Alfred P. Murrah Federal Building and numerous other buildings in the downtown Oklahoma City area.

Larry, whose office was just a few blocks away, was terrified knowing that his wife, Polly, executive director of the Oklahoma Foundation for Excellence, was in her office in the Journal Record Building, directly north of the Murrah Building. The Murrah and Journal Record buildings had been struck with a force of 37 tons and the blast was heard for more than 20 miles.[7]

The entire north face of the Murrah Building collapsed and the Journal Record Building was devastated by the blast. Like hundreds of others, Polly was badly injured by imploding glass. Her body and clothing were torn by shards of flying glass and her throat was severely cut. A person working next to her office carried her down three flights of stairs.

Polly was fortunate to be found quickly by emergency ambulance personnel who slowed her bleeding and rushed her to St. Anthony Hospital. She arrived at the hospital just as medical personnel were responding and was wheeled almost directly into an operating room. Fortunately, Polly's surgeon was one of few in the region with the training and experience to repair the severe trauma to her throat. Although her life was saved, months of rehabilitation remained before she completely regained her health.[8]

In addition to helping his church and seeing his family through times of crises, John made time both before and after his semi-retirement to help others. For example, he served as a director and treasurer of the Oklahoma City Golf and Country Club and was a director for the YMCA of Greater Oklahoma City. When his children were enrolled at Casady School, he served on its board of directors. He was a member of the Beacon Club, the Embassy Club, the Mayfair Club, and the Rotary Club. He also was a member of the Oklahoma City Chamber of Commerce and the Oklahoma City Chapter of

Certified Public Accountants. He was president of both the Young Men's Dinner Club of Oklahoma City and the Economic Club, and was one of 50 founders of the Petroleum Club and served on its board of directors. At the state level he was a member of the Oklahoma Society of Certified Public Accountants and the Oklahoma Independent Petroleum Association.[9]

John and Mary also have been strongly involved in higher education. After Larry enrolled at Princeton University, John served on the development board of the Princeton Theological Seminary for more than 20 years. He also was a director of the College of the Ozarks, a small Presbyterian college at Clarksville, Arkansas. On September 18, 1980, Bethany College in West Virginia honored John with a Doctor of Humanities degree for his contributions to higher education.

In addition, Randolph Macon Woman's College, Mary's alma mater, has been a major recipient of the Nichols' time and energy. John was elected to the board of trustees of Randolph-Macon in 1965 and remained on the board for 25 years, at which time he was elected a trustee emeritus.[10]

John and Mary never forgot their attachment to the University of Oklahoma and have been friends to every president of the University of Oklahoma since the 1940s. John worked diligently to make United States Senator David L. Boren president of the University of Oklahoma and generously supported Boren's efforts to bring the university to the front ranks of American institutions of higher learning. Their gifts have funded major programs in the College of Fine Arts, College of Business, the Bizzell Library, and elsewhere.

The Nichols established the first endowed professorship in the School of Dance in appreciation of its success as one of the top three schools in the country and in admiration of its leadership. The Nichols fund two annual scholarships for ballet stu-

In May, 2002, John was awarded an honorary doctorate degree by his alma mater, the University of Oklahoma. He accepted the high honor at the OU commencement at Memorial Stadium along with NBC newsman Tim Russert, left.

dents and serve on many boards and committees of the College of Fine Arts, including the steering committee of the Indian Ballerina Project. For their efforts in the arts, John and Mary received the Governor's Arts Award in 2000.

For many years, John has actively supported the Price College of Business at OU and served on its Board of Visitors. As a result of a gift from the Nichols, five Nichols Faculty Fellowships are awarded each year in the College of Business. In 1993, John was selected as the first "Arthur Barto Adams Alumni Fellow."

In the 1990s, the Nichols helped organize and conduct three International Business and Arts Conferences, which brought together OU faculty and alumni in tours to Vienna, Austria, London, England, and Stockholm, Sweden.

John and Mary are charter members of the Bizzell Library's Board of Visitors of which John served as president. Mary was a member of the first Board of Visitors for OU's *World Literature Today* and a member of the OU Associates Council.

The Nichols served on the Reach for Excellence committee and provided funds for the Sam Noble Oklahoma Museum of Natural History at OU. They have provided scholarships for students both at OU and at other institutions of higher learning, including Austin Presbyterian Theological Seminary, Randolph Macon Woman's College, and the College of the Ozarks.

University of Oklahoma President David L. Boren confers an honorary doctorate degree on John at commencement ceremonies in 2002.

To John Nichols — Congratulations to a great Sooner! David Boren

ABOVE: In 2003, John received the first TrailBlazer Award from the University of Oklahoma. At the ceremony were, left to right, Polly Nichols, Larry Nichols, Kent Nichols, John, Betty Street, David Street, and Mary Nichols.

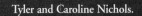

Tyler and Caroline Nichols.

ABOVE: Jeff and Sally Starling.

ABOVE: Rachel and Jeff Street.

RIGHT: Randy and Holly Street.

ABOVE: Kent and Diane Nichols' three daughters, left to right, Laurie, Holly, and Kelly.

BELOW: John and Mary and six of their seven great grandchildren. Left to right, Laurie Street, Ben Graham, Sarah Street, Charlotte Graham, Julie Street, and Jack Graham.

RIGHT: Ethan
Street, the youngest
of the Nichols great
grandchildren.

John and Mary Nichols—still happy after 67 years together.

EPILOGUE

· ·

In 2001, John's pivotal role in the history of the oil and gas industry was recognized in a special supplement produced by Hart Publications, publishers of *Oil and Gas Investor*, entitled "100 Most Influential People of the Petroleum Century." One of only seven listed in a section on "deal-makers," John was recognized for creating the first public oil and gas drilling fund to be registered with the Securities and Exchange Commission, which the magazine characterized as John's "drilling fund brainchild."[1]

An exceptional innovator, shrewd entrepreneur, generous philanthropist, devoted father, loving husband, and one of the most significant 20th century figures in the oil and gas industry, John Nichols built his career on competency, honesty, salesmanship, deep religious faith, and his willingness to take carefully calculated risks. His ability to communicate with and earn the trust of many of the business and financial leaders of America and Europe was essential to the success of Blackwood & Nichols, Devon Resources, and Devon Energy. Moreover, his pioneering innovations in financing oil and gas operations had a dramatic, worldwide impact on the energy industry.

Looking back, John gives credit for his success to his belief in God. John has strictly adhered to the Biblical principle of tithing, giving the first 10 percent of earnings to his church. Each day of his life, he has prayed to God for direction—about decisions concerning both his personal and business life.

Many times John saw opportunity where other people saw problems. With optimism he formed new companies, raising money in the United States and Europe with no fear of debt. "I would borrow anything anyone would lend me," Nichols says with a laugh. "I was just cocky enough to think I could make any project work."[2] And when a project did not work, he turned to the next one, still filled with optimism, on occasion remarking that "Babe Ruth didn't hit a home run every time." To the great benefit of his family, his investors, his employees, his city, higher education, various civic causes, and the energy industry, John's many home runs greatly exceeded his strikeouts.

Larry Nichols summed up his father's business principles in a 1995 speech to an Oklahoma City meeting of The Newcomen Society of the United States. Larry said:

> Devon has come a long way…And yet, Devon is still exactly where we were when we started. It still has all the characteristics John Nichols gave it. We are optimistic about our future, creative in solving our problems, resourceful in exploiting our opportunities, and above all else, honest in our dealings with everyone.[3]

And so, the legacy of John W. Nichols lives on.

APPENDIX

BUSINESSES IN WHICH JOHN W. NICHOLS WAS A PRINCIPAL OWNER OR OFFICER

1950 - 2004

Prepared from corporate records and records in the
office of the Oklahoma Secretary of State.

BLACKWOOD & NICHOLS COMPANY

Formed with F.G. "Blackie" Blackwood in 1950—
an informal partnership engaged in the exploration and development
of oil and gas leases in Oklahoma, Texas, and New Mexico.

BANK OF MIDAMERICA SAVINGS TRUST COMPANY

In 1952, Bill Whiteman and others joined JWN
to set up this entity, which was later purchased by Liberty
National Bank and Trust Company.

FHN, LTD.

In 1957, JWN, Bill Hilsewick, and John Fisher
formed this corporation to hold a majority of their oil and
gas interests formerly held by Blackwood & Nichols.

BLACKWOOD & NICHOLS COMPANY, LTD.

Formed in 1957 to hold the 25 % working interest
in theNortheast Blanco Unit in New Mexcico.

JOHN W. NICHOLS COMPANY, LTD.

In 1956, JWN formed this Oklahoma limited
partnership to engage in oil and gas exploration.

MID-AMERICA MINERALS, INC.
On January 6, 1958, with Bill Hilsewick, Bill Little,
Alex Nason, Cal Stuckeman, and others, JWN created this
corporation to develop oil and gas properties.

LIBERTY NATIONAL BANK AND TRUST COMPANY
In 1960, this bank bought Bank of MidAmerica Savings
Trust Company, making JWN a shareholder in the bank.
In 1962, JWN and John Kirkpatrick purchased
17 % of the stock of the bank.

PASTEUR MEDICAL BUILDING CORPORATION
In 1962, JWN purchased shares in the company that owned the
Pasteur Medical Building in Oklahoma City and bought shares in
Liberty National Bank. PMBC had been incorporated in 1949.

TAU, INC.
Corporation purchased in 1963 that held
controlling interest in Sahara Oilfield Services.

SAHARA OILFIELD SERVICES LTD. ,S.A.
A Panamanian corporation, formed in 1959, purchased
by PMBC in 1963—distributed oilfield equipment in Libya.

SAHARA OILFIELD SERVICES COMPANY OF LIBYA
The Libyan entity that held 51 % of SOS, a division of Essex.

CALVERT EXPLORATION COMPANY
In 1965, Mid-America Minerals, Inc., merged with this
company. Mid-America was a subsidiary until 1969.

PACIFIC PROPERTIES
In 1965, Art Wood and others joined JWN to form this company
to develop real estate, including a television station, in Hawaii.

NICHOLS OPERATIONS, LTD.
Limited partnership formed January 1, 1965.

ESSEX CORPORATION
On December 7, 1965, Pasteur Medical Building Corporation became Essex Corporation.

OFFSHORE DRILLING SUPPLIES LTD.
A United Kingdom corporation founded by Mike Robertson that sold drilling supplies in the North Sea. Purchased in 1965.

LUCEY PRODUCTS CORPORATION
In July, 1965, PMBC purchased this oilfield supply company, founded in 1926.

TRANS-AFRICA ENGINEERING LIMITED
On December 29, 1965, this subsidiary of Essex was formed to coordinate activities in Africa.

TELEVISION BROADCASTERS, INC.
Corporation which owned television station in Beaumont, Texas, was purchased in January, 1966.

PATHFINDER OIL TOOL COMPANY
This company that made oilfield equipment was acquired on April 1, 1966, and became a division of Essex.

EAGLEAIR, INC.
JWN bought all stock of this corporation in December, 1966. The corporation owned an Aero Commander airplane.

SONAX CORPORATION
Organized in 1966, this subsidiary of Essex sold and installed alarm and background music systems.

LIBERTY CORPORATION
A subsidiary of Essex that held Liberty National Bank stock, television station in Beaumont, and Pasteur Medical Building. Formed July 28, 1967.

ESSPLY LIMITED

This United Kingdom corporation, a subsidiary of Essex, was formed on May 24, 1967, to furnish tubular goods to Esso in Europe and Africa.

OIL CO INTERNATIONAL

A subsidiary of Essex created in 1967 with George Daley in charge.

OIL CO EUROPE

A subsidiary of Essex created in 1967 with Ted Findeiss in charge

ESS-MEX, S.A

A Mexican corporation created on September 18, 1967, to import oilfield supplies to Mexico.

PASCO, INC.

An Oklahoma corporation formed in 1967 to distribute holdings of Essex.

L-C INVESTMENT CORPORATION

A successor to Liberty Corporation, formed in 1968.

LIBERTY PROPERTIES, LTD.

In June, 1968, this entity was formed to purchase the old Liberty National Bank Building.

SABINE BROADCASTING COMPANY, INC.

A Texas corporation formed in 1968 to operate the Beaumont television station.

SENECA FUNDS, INC.

Formed with Karl Martin, Jr., Davis Jenkins, and Robert Heston in 1969 to raise money for oil and gas development.

OKAY CORPORATION

Incorporated on July 25, 1969, Okay was a holding company for remaining assets of Essex after sale to Daley. The primary asset was a huge loss carry forward. Merged with Devon Corporation in 1971.

SENECA OIL COMPANY
A Delaware corporation, formed in 1969, was General Partner in Seneca Funds exploration.

EMPRESS GAS LIMITED
A United Kingdom corporation created in 1969 to explore in England.

SENECA 1970 FUND, LTD.
An Oklahoma limited partnership, created November 17, 1969, between Seneca Funds, Inc. and JWN.

OKAY 1970 SOLID MINERAL FUNDS, LTD.
Okay Corporation was General Partner of this Oklahoma limited partnership formed in 1970.

DEVON CORPORATION
An Oklahoma corporation formed on February 20, 1970.

PALOMAR FINANCIAL CORPORATION
Company set up in October, 1970, to purchase Liberty Corporation shares from Okay Corporation.

NICHOLS OPERATIONS LTD.
Oklahoma limited partnership formed in 1970 to explore and develop oil and gas properties.

DEVON RESOURCE INVESTORS
Partnership organized in 1970. Merged with Devon Energy in 1988.

DEVON INTERNATIONAL, S.A.
Luxembourg corporation formed in 1971 to hold royalty interests for European investors.

DEVON INTERNATIONAL ROYALITIES LIMITED
Bermuda corporation formed in 1971 as part of international funding mechanism.

COLDSTREAM PROPERTIES LTD.

A United Kingdom corporation formed in 1971
as part of international funding mechanism.

SAXON OIL COMPANY S.A.

A Panamanian corporation formed in 1971 as part
of international funding mechanism.

TRIDENT ROYALTY CORPORATION

Oklahoma corporation formed in 1971 to hold federal leases.

DEVON-SMEDVIG 1973 OIL & GAS PROGRAM, LTD.

Limited partnership formed in 1973 between Devon
and Smedvig. Merged with Devon Energy in 1988.

FALCO HOLDING COMPANY

Created on June 13, 1974, this company held ownership of Falco,
Inc. and J.E. Fowler Petroleum Products, Inc.

SURREY BROADCASTING COMPANY

Corporation formed in 1975 to own broadcasting stations
in Arizona and Oklahoma.

MID-AMERICA PLAZA, LTD.

An Oklahoma limited partnership formed on September17, 1979,
to acquire Mid-America Tower.

KATT COMMUNICATIONS

Formed in 1981 to own KATT-FM in Oklahoma City.

DEVON ENERGY CORPORATION

Nevada corporation formed on March 25, 1981. Later became
wholly-owned subsidiary of Devon Corporation (Oklahoma).

DEVON ENERGY CORPORATION

A Delaware corporation formed on September 28, 1988,
a public company.

Acquired Northstar on December 19, 1998.

Acquired PennzEnergy on August 17, 1999.

Acquired Santa Fe Snyder on August 29, 2000.

Acquired Concho Resources on June 22, 2001.

Acquired Anderson Energy on October 15, 2001.

Acquired Mitchell Energy in January, 2002.

Acquired Ocean Energy in April, 2003.

NICHOLS INVESTMENT COMPANY

Formed in 1992 to hold title to Laguna Beach house.

NICHOLS HOLDING COMPANY

Formed in 1992 as general partner in Laguna Beach house.

CARIBOU COMMUNICATIONS

Katt Communications changed its name in 1993.

DEVON ENERGY CORPORATION

Oklahoma corporation formed in June, 1995, to take advantage
of franchise tax structure in Oklahoma.

DEVON ENERGY CORPORATION

Delaware corporation formed in 1999 after PennzEnergy
acquisition. In 2004, Devon operated from this corporate entity.

NOTES

·················

one / Ardmore Beginnings

1. Interviews with John Whiteman Nichols in 1996, 2000, and 2002, collectively referred to as John W. Nichols interview, Heritage Archives, Oklahoma City, Oklahoma.

2. Ibid.

3. Randall Hargett Street, *The Ancestors and Descendants of John Whiteman Nichols and Mary* (Davis) Nichols (Oklahoma City: privately published, 1997), p. 37, hereafter referred to as Randy Street, Nichols Ancestors.

4. John Nichols interview.

5. *The History of Carter County* (Fort Worth, Texas: University Supply and Equipment Company, 1975), unpaged.

6. Randy Street, Nichols Ancestors, p. 35.

7. Ibid.; Bob Burke, *These Be Thine Arms Forever* (Oklahoma City: Commonwealth Press, 1993), p. 28.

8. Kenny A. Franks, *Ragtown: A History of the Greater Healdton-Hewitt Oil Field* (Oklahoma City: Oklahoma Heritage Association, 1986), p. 3.

9. Ibid., p. 4.

10. Ibid., p. 5.

11. John Nichols interview.

12. Ibid.

13. Ibid.

14. Ibid.

15. Ibid.

two / Off to College

1. John Nichols interview.

2. Bob Burke, *Good Guys Wear White Hats,* (Oklahoma City: Oklahoma Heritage Association, 2000), p. 24-26.

3. Ibid.

4. Bob Burke and Louise Painter, *Justice Served: The Life of Alma Bell Wilson,* (Oklahoma City: Oklahoma Heritage Association, 2001), p. 43.

5. John Nichols interview.

6. Ibid.

7. Ibid.

8. Ibid.

9. Ibid.

three / Along Came Mary

1. John Nichols interview.

2. A series of interviews with Mary Davis Nichols in 2000, 2001, and 2002, hereinafter referred to as Mary Nichols interview, Heritage Archives.

3. Bob Burke, *Good Guys Wear White Hats*, p. 21.

4. Mary Nichols interview.

5. Ibid.

6. John Nichols interview.

four / Gigolo in Paris

1. Diary of John Nichols, written during 1936 trip to Europe, Heritage Archives, hereinafter referred to as John Nichols diary.

2. Ibid.

3. Ibid.

4. Ibid.

5. Ibid.

6. John Nichols interview.

7. Ibid.

five / Courtship and Marriage

1. Mary Nichols interview.

2. Ibid.; Randy Street, Nichols Ancestors, p. 7.

3. John Nichols interview.

4. Mary Nichols interview.

5. John Nichols interview.

six / Blackwood & Nichols

1. John Nichols interview.

2. Royalty deed found in the files of Devon

Corporation, Heritage
Archives.

3. Ibid.

4. www.utexas.edu

5. John Nichols interview.

6. Ibid.

7. Ibid.

8. Ibid.

9. Ibid.

10. Ibid.

11. Ibid.

12. Ibid.

13. Ibid.

seven / A Winning Team

1. John Nichols interview.

2. Ibid.

3. Prospectus dated
November 28, 1950,
Heritage Archives.

4. Ibid.

5. Ibid.

6. Truman E. Anderson, Jr.
Oil Program Investments.
(Tulsa: Petroleum
Publishing Company,
1972), p. 213.

7. Ibid.

8. John Nichols interview.

9. Ibid.

10. Ibid.

11. Ibid.

**eight / The Lure
of Tax Breaks**

1. John Nichols interview.

2. Interview with John
Fisher, October, 1997,
Heritage Archives.

3. John Nichols interview.

4. Ibid.

5. Ibid.

6. Ibid.

7. Ibid.

8. Ibid.

9. Ibid.

**nine / Diversified
Investments**

1. John Nichols interview.

2. Ibid.

3. Ibid.

4. Ibid.

5. Ibid.

6. Ibid.

ten / S.O.S.

1. John Nichols interview.

2. Ibid.

3. Ibid.

4. Ibid.

5. Ibid.

eleven / Essex

1. Letter from George Daley
to John Nichols, October
18, 1965, Heritage
Archives.

2. Letter from John Nichols
to shareholders, November
1, 1965, Heritage
Archives.

3. John Nichols interview.

4. Letter from George Daley
to John Nichols, May 27,
1966, Heritage Archives.

5. Interview with Michael
Huntley-Robertson,
May 10, 2004, hereafter
referred to as Michael
Robertson interview.

6. Ibid.

7. Ibid.

8. Interview with Dorothy
McDonald, October 17,
1996, Heritage Archives.

9. Corporate records of Essex
Corporation, Heritage
Archives.

10. John Nichols interview.

11. Ibid.

12. Ibid.

twelve / A Family Affair

1. Mary Nichols interview.

2. Ibid.

3. John Nichols interview.

4. Larry Nichols interview.

5. Ibid.

6. Ibid.

7. Ibid.

8. Ibid.

9. Ibid.

10. Interview with Betty Ann
Nichols Street, August 5,
1996, and June 9, 2004,
hereafter referred to as
Betty Street interview,
Heritage Archives.

11. Ibid.

12. Ibid.

13. Mary Nichols interview.

14. Betty Street interview.

15. Ibid.

16. Ibid.

17. Interview with David
Street, August 5, 1996,
hereafter referred to as
David Street interview,
Heritage Archives.

18. Ibid.

19. Interview with James
Kent Nichols, August 5,
1996, and June 25, 2004,
hereafter referred to as
Kent Nichols interview,
Heritage Archives.

20. Ibid.

21. Ibid.

22. Ibid.

23. Ibid.

24. Ibid.

25. Ibid.

26. Ibid.

27. Ibid.

28. Ibid.

29. Ibid.

thirteen / A New Name

1. Larry Nichols interview.
2. John Nichols interview.
3. Ibid.
4. Interview with Gary Fuller, March 10, 2004, hereinafter referred to as Gary Fuller interview, Heritage Archives.
5. Ibid.
6. Ibid.
7. John Nichols interview.
8. Interview with John van Merkensteijn, III, January 20, 2004, hereafter referred to as John van Merkensteijn interview, Heritage Archives.
9. Ibid.
10. Ibid.
11. Ibid.

fourteen / European Investors

1. Interview with Norman Benzaquen, January 20, 2004, hereinafter referred to as Norman Benzaquen interview, Heritage Archives.
2. Ibid.
3. Ibid.
4. Interview with Peter Grunebaum, January 20, 2004, hereinafter referred to as Peter Grunebaum interview, Heritage Archives.
5. Ibid.
6. Ibid.
7. Ibid.
8. Ibid.
9. Ibid.
10. Ibid.
11. Ibid.
12. Ibid.

13. Ibid.
14. Ibid.
15. Interview with Gary Fuller, May 22, 1996, Heritage Archives.
16. John Nichols interview.
17. Norman Benzaquen interview.
18. Ibid.
19. Larry Nichols interview.
20. Letter from Susan Ketch to author, April 14, 2004, Heritage Archives.
21. Ibid.

fifteen / A Partnership with P & O

1. www.pohub.com, official Website of the Peninsular and Oriental Steam Navigation Company.
2. Interview with Michael K. Taylor, January 30, 2004, hereafter referred to as Michael Taylor interview, Heritage Archives.
3. Ibid.
4. Report to P & O prepared by Michael K. Taylor, May 5, 1972, Heritage Archives.
5. Michael Taylor interview.
6. Ibid.
7. Ibid.
8. Ibid.
9. John Nichols interview.
10. Ibid.
11. Ibid.
12. Ibid.
13. Larry Nichols interview.
14. John Nichols interview.
15. Ibid.
16. Larry Nichols interview.
17. Ibid.
18. Ibid.

19. Michael Robertson interview.
20. Ibid.
21. Ibid.
22. Michael Taylor interview.
23. Larry Nichols interview.
24. Ibid.
25. John Nichols interview.
26. Larry Nichols interview.
27. John Nichols interview.
28. Larry Nichols interview.
29. Michael Taylor interview.
30. Devon Energy Corporation, Annual Report, 1974, Heritage Archives.

sixteen / Major Expansion

1. Peter Grunebaum interview.
2. John Nichols interview.
3. Larry Nichols interview.
4. Ibid.
5. Michael Taylor interview.
6. Gary Fuller interview.
7. Ibid.
8. Michael Taylor interview.
9. John Nichols interview.
10. Interview with Thomas Fenton Ferguson, June 7, 2004, Heritage Archives.
11. Ibid.
12. Ibid.
13. Larry Nichols interview.
14. W. David Baird and Danney Goble, *The Story of Oklahoma* (Norman: University of Oklahoma Press, 1994), p. 479-480.
15. Larry Nichols interview.
16. Ibid.
17. Devon Energy Corporation Annual Report, 1995, Heritage Archives.

seventeen / Devon Energy

1. John Nichols interview.
2. Ibid.
3. Ibid.
4. Interview with Terry Barrett, May 23, 1996, Heritage Archives.
5. Ibid.
6. John Nichols interview.
7. Larry Nichols interview.
8. Ibid.
9. John Nichols interview.
10. Ibid.
11. Larry Nichols interview.
12. Ibid.
13. Ibid.
14. Ibid.
15. Ibid.
16. Ibid.
17. *The Daily Oklahoman* (Oklahoma City, Oklahoma), August 24, 1989.
18. Devon Energy Corporation, Annual Report, 1991, Heritage Archives.

eighteen / Aggressive Expansion

1. *The Daily Oklahoman*, July 3, 1992.
2. *Ibid.*, May 19, 1994; Devon Energy Corporation, Annual Report, 1994, Heritage Archives.
3. *The Daily Oklahoman*, June 6, 1995.
4. Ibid., January 1, 1997; Larry Nichols interview.
5. Ibid.
6. Devon Energy Corporation, Annual Report, 1996, Heritage Archives.
7. *The Daily Oklahoman*, October 19, 1997.
8. Devon Energy Corporation, Annual Report, 1997, Heritage Archives.
9. *The Daily Oklahoman*, April 26, 1998.
10. Ibid.
11. *Fortune* (New York, New York), September 29, 1998.
12. *The Daily Oklahoman*, March 1, 1999.
13. Ibid., August 18, 1999.
14. Ibid.
15. *Wall Street Journal* (New York, New York), August 13, 1999.
16. *The Daily Oklahoman*, August 30, 2000.
17. *Wall Street Journal*, August 18, 2000.
18. Larry Nichols interview.
19. *The Sunday Oklahoman* (Oklahoma City, Oklahoma), October 15, 2000.
20. *The Daily Oklahoman*, September 27, 2000.
21. Ibid., October 15, 2000.
22. Ibid., May 18, 2001.
23. Ibid., September 22, 2001.
24. Ibid., September 22, 2001.
25. Ibid., August 15, 2001.
26. Ibid., January 24, 2002.
27. Ibid.
28. *Friday* (Oklahoma City, Oklahoma), March 7, 2003.
29. *The Daily Oklahoman*, October 28, 2001.
30. Ibid., January 25, 2002.

nineteen / Giving Back to Oklahoma

1. Letter from Jack H. Abernathy to Oklahoma Heritage Association, April 17, 1986, Heritage Archives.
2. Oklahoma Hall of Fame File of John W. Nichols, Heritage Archives.
3. John Nichols interview.
4. Larry Nichols interview.
5. Ibid.
6. John Nichols interview.
7. *The Daily Oklahoman*, April 20, 1995.
8. John Nichols interview.
9. Ibid.
10. Ibid.

Epilogue

1. *100 Most Influential People of the Petroleum Century*, 2001, p. 66.
2. John Nichols interview.
3. Printed remarks of Larry Nichols at The Newcomen Society of the United States meeting in Oklahoma City, June 28, 1995, Heritage Archives.

BIBLIOGRAPHY &
SUGGESTED READING

Blackburn, Bob L. *Heart of the Promised Land—Oklahoma County.* Woodland Hills, California: Windsor Publications, Inc., 1982.

Brossard, E.B. Petroleum, Politics and Power. Tulsa: PennWell Books, 1983.

Burke, Bob. *Oklahoma—The Center of It All. Encino, California:* Cherbo Publishing, 2002.

Connelly, W.L. The Oil Business as I Saw It. Norman: University of Oklahoma Press, 1954.

Franks, Kenny A. *The Oklahoma Petroleum Industry.* Norman: University of Oklahoma Press, 1980.

Franks, Kenny A., Paul F. Lambert, and Carl N. Tyson, *Early Oklahoma Oil.* College Station: Texas A & M Press, 1981.

Lambert, Paul F., Kenny A. Franks, and Bob Burke. *Historic Oklahoma: An* Illustrated History. San Antonio: Lammert Publications, Inc., 2000.

Stewart, Roy P., with Pendleton Wood. Born Grown. Oklahoma City: Fidelity Bank, 1974.

INDEX